BERLITZ®

JERUSALEM

How to use our guide

- All the practical information, hints and tips that you will need before and during the trip start on page 103.

- For general background, see the sections The City and the People, p.6, and A Brief History, p. 12.

- All the sights to see are listed between pages 22 and 68, with suggestions for daytrips from Jerusalem from page 70 to 84 and on page 102. Our own choice of sights most highly recommended is pinpointed by the ☑ Berlitz symbol.

- Entertainment, nightlife and all other leisure activities are described between pages 85 and 93, while information on restaurants and cuisine is to be found on pages 94 to 101.

- Finally, there is an index at the back of the book, pp. 126–128.

Although we make every effort to ensure the accuracy of the information in this book, changes occur incessantly. We cannot therefore take responsibility for facts, addresses and circumstances in general that are constantly subject to alteration. If you have any new information, suggestions or corrections to contribute, we would like to hear from you. Please write to Berlitz Publishing at the address on page 2.

Text: Tom Brosnahann
Photography: Erling Mandelmann
Layout: Aude Aquoise
We are particularly grateful to Ronald Miller for his help in the preparation of this book. We also wish to thank Mrs J. Zakkak, the Israel Government Tourist Office and El Al Israel Airlines for their valuable assistance.

Cartography: 🅕 Falk-Verlag, Hamburg.

Contents

The City and the People

No matter how extravagant your expectations, Jerusalem can fulfil them. Holy City to Jews, Christians and Moslems, capital of modern Israel, dynamic metropolis, Jerusalem succeeds in being most things to most people.

Above all, it is a city for visitors, and in a very real sense a second home to every Jew, Christian and Moslem in the world. Though it may take a while to get accustomed to the Old City's lacework of lanes and alleys and to sort out the Judean hills and dales, from your first moment in Jerusalem you will feel that you know the place in spirit and that you belong.

Jerusalemites of every faith are eager to make visitors welcome, whatever the reason for their trip. You can watch a group of black-bearded Orthodox Jews shepherding sons and grandsons to the venerable Western Wall for prayer, or stop and enjoy the sonorous chanting of the muezzing who call the faithful to noontime devotions from the minaret of El-Aksa Mosque; or visit the Franciscan monks, who will explain the significance of the fourteen Stations of the Cross along the Via Dolorosa. After a tiring day's pilgrimage and sightseeing, you can relax in Jerusalem's comfortable hotels, hospices and restaurants.

Despite the friendly welcome, the city lives its history every day. Mutual respect is usually the rule among the many denominations and sects of the three great religions, but this is sacred ground and has had more blood spilled on it for its own sake than

Reverence for tradition and zest for life; a bar mitzvah at the Western Wall, and a comely smile.

any other place in the world. Rivalries lie dormant and do not disappear. Don't be surprised to find a soldier, submachine gun slung across his shoulder, seated watchfully in a bus, a café or a park; it is this kind of vigilance that keeps the city peaceful.

Being at the centre of the religious world brings a bewildering diversity to life in Jerusalem. A dozen languages echo from the dome above the Church of the Holy Sepulchre, and some of the shopkeepers in the labyrinthine bazaars speak all of them and more. Nowhere else on earth are you likely to see such a variety of costumes. Hassidic Jews wear black hats surrounded by fur, and long black or brocaded coats, the garb dating from the origin of their sect in 18th-century eastern Europe. Arabs are clad in flowing robes and *keffiyes* (head scarves), or jackets and fezzes, or blue jeans and T-shirts. Nuns are in their habits, tourists in Bermuda shorts, Israeli women in military uniforms, berobed Orthodox priests and Bedouin women in richly embroidered dresses.

To whom does Jerusalem belong? In spirit, it's everyone's.

These colourful contrasts are further enriched by the thousands of Jews who have moved to the Promised Land since the founding of modern Israel in 1948.

Since that year hundreds of thousands of immigrants, displaced persons, refugees and survivors of the Nazi holocaust have been offered sanctuary in the new state. Despite difficult political and economic conditions for everyone, determination plus the application of modern techniques to the economy provided all of them with a roof over their heads and enough to eat.

The population of Israel is just over 5 million, of whom some 4,144,500 are Jews, 701,400 Moslems and 128,000 Christians. There are also over 50,000 Druze – members of a religious sect which broke away from Islam in the 11th century – most of whom live in Galilee and Mount Carmel.

The Jewish people in Israel are from many lands, and differ in culture, garb and features. Some have lived in Israel for generations, but most have arrived from every part of the world since 1948: Ashkenazim from Europe – among them the mystical Hassidim who worship God with **9** song and dance; Sephardic Jews exiled from Spain in 1492 at the time of the Inquisition; black-eyed, high-cheekboned Yemenite Jews; dark-skinned Cochin Jews from India; Jews from Morocco and Tunisia; Jews from the mountains of Kurdistan; dark, delicate-featured Jews from Ethiopia; and swarms of Soviet Jews. Today, native-born "Sabras" make up more than half of the Israeli Jewish population.

But wherever they come from, and however varied their customs, the Jewish people are united by a religion, a language, a common heritage and history, and a feeling of being one people in their ancestral homeland.

As you plunge into the sights, sounds and colours of this fascinating city, you'll find that planning your day is no easy matter. Each religion has a different Sabbath and a different calendar of religious holidays. A day's itinerary is often confounded as shops, offices, mosques and museums are opened or shut for religious or patriotic festivals, prayers, traditions, or just a summer afternoon's siesta. But if some places close abruptly, others open just as suddenly – Jerusalem is never completely at rest.

In the midst of the confusion is a passion for continuity. Any change, even moving a candlestick, must take into account a hundred beliefs and traditions. By general agreement and city ordinance, all buildings must be

Hebrew University's modern structures echo those of ancient times. Walls of tawny Jerusalem limestone have the look of petrified sunlight.

faced with tawny limestone, keeping the city Jerusalem the Golden. Perhaps this kind of mutual respect and cooperation will be the Holy City's salvation after so many centuries of strife.

11

A Brief History

The Bible is our best source for the history of early Jerusalem. In Bronze Age times, around 1850 B.C., "Urusalim" or "Salem" was ruled by a king called Melchizedek. Genesis tells us that he once blessed Abraham, giving him bread and wine *(Gen. 14:18–20)*. Later, when God made his covenant with Abraham, part of it called for his descendants to conquer many lands. One of them was Canaan, in which lay the city of Urusalim.

In the centuries between 1400 and 1000 B.C., the tribes of Israel conquered all the lands north and south of Jerusalem, leaving the fortified city as the only undefeated spot in the territory. Then, around 1000 B.C., the chiefs of the tribes of Israel elected David, a young man of some 30 years from Bethlehem, to be their king.

The Kingdoms of David and Solomon

Not wanting to set a dangerous precedent by favouring one or another of the tribal towns for the establishment of his court, King David prepared to march on Jerusalem, then called Jebus. He intended to make it his royal city.

Finding out about the Jebusites' water tunnel under the walls, the Israelites slipped into the city and took it by surprise *(2 Sam. 5:8)*.

The king strengthened the walls and the fortress called Zion. He brought in the Ark of the Covenant to make Jerusalem a Holy City. The might of the kingdom grew, and by the time his son Solomon succeeded him around 965 B.C., almost all of the extensive and potentially wealthy lands between the Nile and the Euphrates belonged to Israel.

King Solomon ruled during the Golden Age of Hebrew Jerusalem. The king is remembered not only for his proverbial wisdom, but also for the construction of the First Temple, on land which his father had purchased from the defeated king of the Jebusites. The plot of land was north of the small Davidic city, on top of Mount Moriah (now the site of the Dome of the Rock). Used in earlier times as a threshing-place, it was, legend says, the spot where Abraham's near-sacrifice of Isaac had been made. The First Temple was impressive more for its beauty and elegance than for its size. Along with the splendid house of worship, Solomon built a royal palace, mansions for his wives, barracks for his guards, and towers for the defence of the capital.

But the Golden Age lasted barely a century, from David's conquest to the death of King Solomon. Later monarchs were never able to reign in such power and glory as he had. In 701 B.C. the Assyrian armies of Sennacherib besieged Jerusalem, and it narrowly escaped destruction. The end of David's dynasty came in 587 B.C. when Nebuchadnezzar, King of Babylon, invaded Judah to lay siege to Jerusalem (2 Kings 24, 25). When it fell, the Temple and all the buildings were put to the torch. The people of the once-glorious city were forced into exile.

In time the kingdom of Babylon was overthrown, and the Israelites began to return to Jerusalem. The city was now (539 B.C.) under the more tolerant rule of the Persians. Rebuilding was slow work. The Second Temple was finished in 515 B.C., but much of the city still lay in ruins.

Jerusalem gave in peaceably to the world-rule of Alexander the Great (332 B.C.), and in following centuries to that of the Egyptians and Seleucids as well. Then, in the 2nd century, Jews led by Judas Maccabeus revolted against the Seleucids and restored the primacy of Jewish religious life in Jerusalem. The reconsecration of the Temple, accomplished in 164 B.C., has been commemorated ever since in the ceremonies of Hanukkah (Feast of Dedication). The Hasmoneans, descendants of the Maccabeans, surrounded the city with a wall and towers. They ruled until the coming of Pompey's Roman legions, in 63 B.C.

Romans and Christians

After the initial few years of Roman administration and political infighting, Herod the Great was made King of Judea. He reigned from 40 to 4 B.C. during which time he fortified the Hasmonean wall and rebuilt three of the towers; one still stands. Several palaces were built and a water system installed. Temple Mount was shored up by walls made with great stone blocks. (One of these, the Western Wall, was later to become a symbol of Jewish longings for Jerusalem's vanished greatness.) Herod also rebuilt the Temple, and put up a fortress nearby. He named it Antonia, in honour of his Roman friend and benefactor Mark Antony.

In addition to all the construction work, Herod did everything 13

Jesus shares Passover seder in Giotto's Last Supper *(Padua).*

he could to beautify the city and glorify himself but he never succeeded in getting his subjects to love him. It wasn't surprising, as this was the same Herod the Great, rebuilder of Jerusalem, who ordered the massacre of all newborn babies in an attempt to do away with the heralded Messiah *(Matt. 2:16)*. Joseph and Mary escaped the wrath and paranoia of Herod by fleeing into Egypt with the infant Jesus.

Jesus was born in Bethlehem, Joseph's ancestral home, in about 6 B.C.* After returning from Egypt, his parents lived in Nazareth, but they used to come up to Jerusalem every year for Passover. When Jesus was about thirty years old, he went to be baptized by John, an ascetic preacher living in the wilds of the Jordan valley *(Matt. 3:13–16)*.

Not long afterwards he embarked on a period of travelling and teaching which lasted for about three years. Much of the

---

* The exact year of Jesus' birth is uncertain; most sources give the date as around 6 B.C.

time was spent in Galilee, a province north of Judea, but his influence was so great among the people that even the Temple priests and government officers in Jerusalem knew about his work. Jesus' lessons were simple and matter-of-fact, but they put in question much religious and legal tradition, and were therefore a threat to the priests and secular rulers.

After his years of teaching, Jesus and his followers went to Jerusalem for Passover. The Holy City at this time was a powder-keg of dissatisfaction with Roman domination. Jesus' triumphal entry into the city caused a commotion and soon afterwards he was arrested by the Temple priests *(Luke 22:54)* who were under Roman rule. Jesus was put on trial quickly on Thursday evening and Friday morning by the Sanhedrin, or supreme rabbinical court. The Sanhedrin's members found him guilty of blasphemy for calling himself the Son of God. But no death sentence could be carried out unless confirmed by the Roman procurator, Pontius Pilate. Pilate was in a difficult situation: he could find no evidence against Jesus and wanted to release him, but pressure groups prevented him from doing so. He tried to escape his responsibility by "washing his hands" of the affair *(Matt. 27:24)*, but nevertheless handed over the prisoner in his charge. The sentence was carried out quickly on Friday, before sunset brought the beginning of the Passover Sabbath. On the third day after his death, according to Christian belief, he was resurrected.

Destruction of Jerusalem

After Jesus' crucifixion, the delicate balance of Jewish municipal government under Roman overlordship continued in Jerusalem until A.D. 66 when the city rebelled against the Romans. For four years the Jewish Zealots fought against the might of Rome. At the end, in A.D. 70, Titus the Roman general laid siege to the city, finally attacking its starved and weakened defenders. Those who didn't escape were executed or sold into slavery and the Holy City was totally destroyed. The last of the Zealots held out for another three years at Masada (see p. 75).

For some 60 years Jerusalem lay in ruins, until the Roman Emperor Hadrian rebuilt the town in the 2nd century, naming it Aelia Capitolina. Except for the Jewish revolt of Bar Kokhba (A.D. 132–135), the new town remained relatively peaceful and people lived from day to day with little excitement.

All this changed when the Roman Empire became Christian in the 4th century. Jerusalem suddenly acquired new and great significance. Empress Helena, a Christian and the mother of Constantine the Great, took a particular interest in the city and its holy places. A church was built around Golgotha (the hill where Jesus' crucifixion had taken place), and other spots important to Jesus' life were found and commemorated. Pilgrims came from throughout the Roman (and later, Byzantine) Empire during the centuries which followed, but the prosperity they brought lasted only until 614, when ferocious Persian armies overran Judea and reduced Jerusalem to rubble once more.

Still reeling from the effects of the Persian devastation Jerusalem was conquered soon (638) by the forces of Islam. The city was very important to Moslems, as according to Islam, Mohammed had been summoned by angels while he slept in Mecca and rode a magic steed into the heavens, travelling as far as Jerusalem. The "farthest spot" (in Arabic *El-Aksa*) that he reached was the site of Temple Mount. To this day, the Dome of the Rock, built in 691, remains one of Jerusalem's most striking monuments.

Jerusalem was subject to Moslem rule for most of the years between the 7th and 11th centuries. Then, in 1099, under their leaders Tancred and Godfrey de Bouillon, the Crusaders captured the Holy City for Christendom.

Crusaders, Mamelukes and Turks

The Crusaders established a feudal state with Godfrey at its head. They built many impressive churches during the short term of the first Latin Kingdom of Jerusalem (1099–1187) but were later driven out by the Kurdish Moslem warrior Saladin. Then, in the Sixth Crusade (1228–29), Frederick II, the Holy Roman emperor, managed to secure Jerusalem for the Crusaders by negotiation.

But the Christians couldn't hold the city from the surrounding sea of Islam, and by the mid-13th century the Mamelukes of Egypt had taken complete control of the land, ruling Jerusalem **17** in relative peace for the next two and a half centuries. Much of the best architecture in the city dates from Mameluke times.

In the early 16th century, the Ottomans, a Turkish dynasty which had absorbed the remnants of the Byzantine empire in the 14th and 15th centuries, were extending their power throughout the Middle East. Jerusalem fell to them in 1517 and remained under their control for 400 years.

Suleiman the Magnificent, the powerful Ottoman sultan, took a special interest in Jerusalem, rebuilding the walls and gates in the form they retain to this day. Fountains, inns, religious colleges and barracks were constructed, and the city flourished as long as he was sultan. But when Suleiman died, the great empire began a long period of decline, and Jerusalem declined along with it. For 300 years the Holy City remained a backwater, until the 19th century, when renewed interest among Christian pilgrims made it the goal of thousands of travellers each year.

19th-Century Aspirations and the British Mandate

At this time another group of Europeans was also interested in the

One man's dream inspired the Jewish return to Israel. His name is sufficient epitaph: Herzl.

city and the region. Many Jews sought religious freedom and fulfilment by moving to Palestine, and especially to Jerusalem. In the last decades of the 19th century, Theodor Herzl (1860–1904) worked to organize the Zionist movement whose aim was the formation of a Jewish state. Chaim Weizmann (1874–1952), a scientist born in Russia but later a British subject, did much to put the theories of Herzl into practice. Weizmann was an important figure in the negotiations with the British which ended with the Balfour Declaration in 1917. The declaration supported the idea of a Jewish "national home" in Palestine, with full respect for the rights of the existing non-Jewish peoples already living there, but the problem was that British strategists, who had gained control from the Turks in 1917, had secretly promised the lands to their First World War Arab allies.

In 1922, the League of Nations granted the British a mandate to administer Palestine. It lasted until 1948 during which

time Zionists battled Arab nationalists for control of the territory. Each side had a weighty claim to the land based on history and religion, and each was supported by a part of the British administration. Power plays, legal wrangles and even gun battles broke the peace as both sides fought their opponents and the British overlords. In 1947, the United Nations voted for the partition of Palestine into two states, one Jewish, one Arab, with Jerusalem as an international city that belonged to neither. But lacking the means to enforce its decision, the United Nations was powerless to halt the bitter strife which broke out as the British withdrew their troops in 1948.

Modern Israel

The State of Israel was declared during this difficult time, with Chaim Weizmann as first president. In response, member states of the Arab League sent troops to help the Palestinian Arabs. Jerusalem and the whole region were carved up by battle lines.

Armistice agreements were reached early in 1949. Israel held the land granted by the U.N. decision and the Arab League states received most of the parts once destined to be a Palestinian Arab state. Jerusalem became a divided city: the western portion in Israeli territory, the eastern portion including the Old City and the holy places in Jordanian territory.

In the 20 years that followed, Jerusalem was two cities. Both geographical and human divisions were aggravated by occasional incidents of terrorism or sniping until the Six-Day War in June

Centuries of conquest and construction made Jerusalem the world's grandest architectural museum: skyline testifies to turbulent history.

1967. Within three days the city was completely in Israeli hands, and in two weeks it was physically and administratively reunited.

The continuing saga of Jerusalem's battles, treaties, politics and passions has proved that cultural reunification is more than re- moving barbed wire or breaking down stone walls. The mood in the city is usually something of a cool respect and resignation to the idea of living and working togeth- er. While all Jerusalemites yearn for peace, true brotherhood is for the future, in better days.

What to See

Perhaps the best introduction to Jerusalem is a ride on the No. 99 bus, which shuttles between the major tourist sights. After that, you'll want to set out on foot. You can explore on your own or join a guided walking tour (for routes and times: 24 King George Street, tel. 754888). No one should miss the walk atop the tawny walls that surround the Old City.

We start our tour within the walls, in the ancient centre. (For opening hours, see pp. 120–122.)

 ## The Old City

The Old City is large by medieval standards, but quite small by modern ones. Its streets are narrow, full of twisting lanes, oriental *souks*, steep stairways and dark, covered passageways. It will take you several days before the maze becomes familiar, several more before the principal landmarks become easily identifiable.

A good place to begin is the **Jaffa Gate,** a pair of massive medieval towers which form part of the Citadel of David, prime bastion of the city for thousands of years. Just through the gate is a branch of the Israel Government Tourist Office, and beside it two quaint old Moslem tombs behind an iron fence.

The **Citadel of David** has two entrances, one to the right before you enter Jaffa Gate, and one a short distance along the road through the gate. The latter is the more interesting: built by Suleiman the Magnificent in 1531–32, it bears inscriptions in three varieties of Arabic script, and leads to a bridge over the remains of the Citadel's moat. Take time to mount the stairs to the roof and battlements for views of the city and explore the ruins and excavations. **Tower of David – the Museum of the History of Jerusalem** is set up in the Citadel, with displays outlining the history of the city (see p. 86). In the evening, a dramatic sound-and-light show is held under the stars in the courtyard (see p. 92).

Across the street from the moat entrance to the Citadel is Christ Church, the oldest Anglican church in the Middle East (1849). There are also a few cafés, as well as public services including a bank, post office, telephone kiosk and a police station.

The south-western part of the Old City, surrounding the Citadel

N

Jericho Road

Mary's Tomb

Church of All Nations

1 Tourist Office
2 Church of St. Veronica
3 Our Lady of the Spasm
Armenian Catholic Church
4 Ecce Homo Arch
5 Convent of the Flagellation
6 Tiferet Israel Synagogue
7 Yohanan Ben Zakkai Synagogue
8 Old Yishuv Court Museum
9 Rockefeller Museum

200 m
200 yards
100
100

St. Stephen's Church

Lions' Gate
(St. Stephen's Gate)

Pool of Bethesda

Church of St. Anne

El-Omariye School

Antonia

Golden Gate

Gate of Sultan Suleiman

El-Omariye

Esh Sheikh Hassan

Darwish

MOSLEM

Solomon's Quarries

El-Bustami

El-Mawlawiyeh

Esh Sheikh Rihan

Damascus Gate

QUARTER

Haram es-Sharif

Dome of the Chain

Mt. Moriah (Temple Mount)

Dome of the Rock

El-Kas

El-Aksa Mosque

Solomon's Stables

Ophel

Via Dolorosa

Suk el-Qattanin

Gate of the Chain

Ha-Ofel

Hazanhanim

Notre Dame de France

Ayihhet

Via Dolorosa

El-Wad

Khan ez-Zeit

El-Saraya

El-Taqiyeh

Street of the Chain

Western Wall

Archaeological Excavations

Dung Gate

New Gate

Frères St. François

Church of the Holy Sepulchre

Street of David

CHRISTIAN QUARTER

Casa Nova

St. Dimitri

Christ Church

Cardo

Habad

David

Cathedral of St. James

Armenian Patriarchate

Jaffa Gate

Citadel of David

Jaffa Road

Zahal Square

Shivte Yisrae'

Misgav Ladach

Chayei Olam

Yehuda Hehasid Synagogue

Ramban Synagogue

JEWISH QUARTER

Bate Mahasse

Ararat

ARMENIAN QUARTER

Zion Gate

JERUSALEM – OLD CITY

(I–XIV = Stations of the Cross)

of David, is the **Armenian Quarter** and has been inhabited by this staunch Christian people since early times. Up the hill past the police station, a short distance along the Street of the Armenian Patriarchate, brings you to the **Cathedral of Saint James** and its convent. Visits are allowed to the ancient and mysterious church, but only during afternoon services.

The most direct route from the Jaffa Gate and the Citadel to Temple Mount is by way of the intriguing oriental bazaars along the **Street of David** (as you come through Jaffa Gate, just walk in a straight line to the descending steps). You'll know you're in the right place by the small boys, who hurtle down the narrow street with carts full of vegetables, bolts of cloth, leather goods and sides of mutton. The carts serve shops in the places where larger vehicles can't go; their only brakes are old tires dragged by chains, which the boys step on before the speed becomes murderous.

The **bazaar** is simply fascinating. Souvenir shops abound, their façades draped with carpets and cloths, their interiors piled high with treasures and trash. After examining the glitter and gimcrack-

ery, don't miss a look in the many local shops which give the bazaar much of its character. Spice shops are filled with brimming sacks of fragrant powders and seeds, and at the butcher's your eyes will meet those of a dozen disembodied sheep's heads, ready for the pot. Tailors, cobblers and metalworkers all ply their trades near the din of hagglers in the municipal produce market.

Turn right at the end of the street, through a gateway, into **Cardo Street.** Originally the main street of ancient Jerusalem (*cardo* means "heart"), it dates back to the Byzantine period. After recent careful restoration, the street has been rehabilitated with shops and galleries. The original arches and vaults remain in some parts; other parts of the street are colonnaded: you can see the original 15-foot columns topped by Corinthian capitals.

The Street of David leads into the Street of the Chain (HaShalshelet, Es-Silsila), which goes straight towards Bab es-Silsila, the Gate of the Chain. This is only one of several entrances to the Haram es-Sharif, the "noble enclosure" atop Temple Mount. You can visit Temple Mount daily, but on Friday, the Moslem Sabbath,

Traditional transport is still best in narrow, congested Old City.

and major Moslem holidays the Haram is closed to non-Moslems. (During the holy month of Ramadan special rules apply.)

Temple Mount, or Mount Moriah, where King Solomon built the First Temple and later generations the Second, is holy ground to all three of Jerusalem's great religions. So sacred are the confines of the Temple site that strictly observant Jews dare not even come here, and Moslems and Christians come with great reverence. Solomon's Temple was completed in about 960 B.C., but the Babylonians destroyed it 400 years later. By 515 B.C., Jews under the rule of Cyrus of Persia had built the Second Temple. It was to last for 600 years until it was destroyed by the Romans. **25**

For Moslems, ever since Mohammed stepped upon the rock on Temple Mount, which tradition identifies as Abraham's altar, the place has been El-Haram es-Sharif. The Prophet made the mysterious night-time journey accompanied by a band of angels, mounted upon El-Burak, a miraculous beast. Built right over the celebrated rock in 691, the **Dome of the Rock** (Kubbet es-Sakhra) is Jerusalem's most strikingly beautiful house of worship. Panels of brilliantly coloured tiles and bands of Koranic inscriptions surround the upper part of the octagonal mosque, while marble panels in muted pastel shades offset this brilliance from below. Leave your shoes by the door as you enter.

The richness of the exterior is echoed, even excelled, inside. The rock is surrounded by a richly worked wooden screen, and above it are stained-glass windows and black-and-gold mosaics, simply breathtaking in their beauty. Look carefully at the rock to find Mohammed's footprint, and inspect the small tabernacle

Monument to a miraculous flight: Dome of the Rock blazes with gold and polychrome tilework.

at its southern extremity, which holds several hairs from the Prophet's beard. Underneath the sacred rock is a grotto where, so they say, great prophets and kings of the past came to pray, and the souls of the dead travel for their devotions.

Surrounding the Dome of the Rock are smaller Islamic buildings put up at different times. The **Dome of the Chain** is a miniature copy of the Dome of the Rock. Sabeel Qait Bey, an ornate little 15th-century kiosk, shows the fine design and craftsmanship of the Mameluke period. From it, fresh water was served to mosque visitors in earlier times. By the arches and stairs leading down to El-Aksa Mosque is the pretty Minber of Kadi Burhan ed-Din, a pulpit used in the summer when prayers can be said outdoors.

Pass under the arches and down the steps to El-Aksa Mosque. Note the sundial at the centre top of the archway. It's accurate to within about five minutes, and has the advantage of needing no winding, though it does "stop" on cloudy days.

Further down, you pass two places reserved for the ritual ablutions which must be performed by Moslems before prayers. One is a circular fountain with a pool, fitted at the bottom with spigots and seats and called El-Kas ("The Cup").

The caliph El-Walid built the first **El-Aksa** (715) on the site of an earlier holy place but earthquakes destroyed it. In 1034 it was rebuilt, basically in the form it has today. The Crusaders used it as a church, but when Saladin conquered Jerusalem, El-Aksa became a mosque once more.

The structure is imposing from the outside, and affects you even more once you've slipped off your shoes and entered the great cool interior. Mammoth marble pillars support beams and a ceiling painted in coloured arabesque; the floor is graced by oriental carpets with intricate patterns. Stained-glass windows, worshippers at prayer, and a holy man reading to himself from the Koran add to the calm and peaceful atmosphere. Be careful not to walk in front of those at prayer. At the far end of the mosque the pillars are of precious breccia and chalcedony and the stone work in the *mihrab* (prayer niche) has delicate carvings.

East of El-Aksa is a large open pavement, underneath which lie tremendous vaulted chambers called Solomon's Stables. You have to find a guide and pay an extra fee to visit this dingy, man-made cavern. From the far eastern corner in the wall is a marvellous **view** of the Mount of Olives and the Garden of Gethsemane plus the ancient tombs in the Kidron Valley. Tradition says that this corner is the "Pinnacle of the Temple" where Jesus was brought by Satan during his temptation *(Matt. 4:5)*.

El Aksa's opulent interior: the carpets alone are worth a fortune.

Just below the Dome of the Rock and El-Aksa is the **Western Wall** ("Wailing Wall") of Temple Mount: the most revered place of the Jews. Since the Second Temple's destruction and banishment of the Jews in A.D. 70, Jews have come here to pray and to weep at the loss of the House of God. and to hope for the restitution of Jerusalem to the Jews. When that hope was realized in June 1967, old buildings which crowded the Wall were demolished and a wide plaza was constructed to accommodate the hundreds of worshippers who arrived daily. Whatever your beliefs you'll feel a sense of

awe when approaching the giant stone ashlars (blocks) which supported the foundations of the Temple, and which represent for the Jewish people a promise and a dream come true.

The ashlars of the Prayer Place date from the time of Herod the Great, with later constructions of smaller blocks higher up. This is only a small section of the Western Wall, which overall extends from one side of Temple Mount to the other and is sunk deeply in the rubble-filled earth.

Separate sections of the Wall are reserved for male and female worshippers. Men must have head coverings and women must not have bare shoulders or short skirts when entering the enclosure of the Prayer Place. Skullcaps and shawls are lent free of charge to those who need them.

The gate in the city walls nearest Temple Mount has the unusual name of Dung Gate (Shaar HaAshpot), probably due to the activities of the city's waste collection men in ancient times. There's a first aid station at the southern end of the Wall.

Giant ashlars fitted with precision recall the Temple's glory.

Bordering the plaza at the Western Wall is Old Jerusalem's **Jewish Quarter,** much damaged during the fighting in 1948. The area was in Jordanian hands until reclaimed by Israeli forces in 1967. Since then, reconstruction has been rapid, with new and distinguished houses, shops and synagogues lining every street. Wandering through the Jewish Quarter on a Saturday is the best way to tiptoe back into its history. Among the ruins, some going back to the 1st century B.C., black-clad Hassidic Jews lead children to synagogue or *yeshivas* (schools) for Sabbath study. No less active on weekdays, the quarter includes a centre for writers called Artists' House, artists' galleries and studios, shops, restaurants and cafés.

The **Ramban Synagogue** on Rehov HaYehudim, is the oldest house of worship still standing in the quarter, and was built by Rabbi Moshe Nahmanides when he reestablished the Jewish community here in 1267. Right next to the Ramban is the **Yehuda HeHasid Synagogue,** also called HaHurva or Beit Yaakov, built on the ruins of the 13th-century Crusader Church of St. Martin. Rabbi Yehuda led a thousand of his Polish followers to the Holy City in 1699 and shortly afterwards began construction of the synagogue. Finally completed only in 1864, it was the centre of Ashkenazi worship in the city until the fighting of 1948 when the building was demolished and it became a ruin once more.

The **Yohanan Ben Zakkai Synagogue** is actually four synagogues in one. Finished in 1586, it was the centre of Sephardic worship for centuries. The largest room gives the complex its name. As little decoration was left in these buildings by 1967, furnishings from abandoned Italian synagogues have been used.

The **Tiferet Israel Synagogue,** also called Nisan Bek, was dedicated just over a century ago at a spot off Misgav Ladach and Chayei Olam streets. Though it was not hallowed by time and the prayers of worshippers like its neighbours, Tiferet Israel was the tallest and perhaps the grandest synagogue in late 19th-century Jerusalem. Destroyed in the 1948 war, it is now being rebuilt.

For a look at what it was like to live in the Jewish Quarter during the 19th century, pay a visit to the **Old Yishuv Court Museum** (see p. 87).

Via Dolorosa and the Moslem Quarter

The Way of the Cross, or Via Dolorosa, holds a fascination for visitors to Jerusalem no matter what their beliefs. Though you can reach the starting-point of the walk along the Stations of the Cross by various routes, a stroll through the Moslem Quarter is a picturesque introduction to the Jerusalem of early Christian times.

Begin at **Damascus Gate** (Shaar Shechem, Bab el-Amud) in the Old City's northern wall, the most impressive of all of Jerusalem's gates, and the work of Suleiman the Magnificent's 16th-century masons and builders. Recent excavations uncovered its 2nd-century predecessor, just below it to the left – now the focus of the Roman Gate Museum.

A centre for Arab money-changers lies inside Damascus Gate. Don't expect to see heaps of gold and silver or delicately balanced scales, for they've long been replaced by paper notes and pocket calculators.

Medieval grandeur of Damascus Gate dominates northern wall of Old City: can he capture it?

Through the great gate and down a flight of steps are the busy bazaar streets. Take the street **El-Wad.** Souvenir and jewellery shops are used to foreign tourists, so be prepared for proprietors who look upon it as a special treat whenever a foreigner drops in.

Turn left into the Via Dolorosa and walk along to the eastern end to the **Lions' Gate,** or St. Stephen's Gate, built in Sultan Suleiman's time. According to the legend, the great Sultan was threatened in a dream by two lions who told him to see to the rebuilding of Jerusalem's dilapidated walls. He rebuilt them quickly and magnificently, transferring his visionary antagonists to a place of honour on this handsome gate. Stop here to admire the **view** of the Kidron Valley, and the Mount of Olives on the other side of it, with the Garden of Gethsemane a green patch on the mountain side, and ancient Jewish cemeteries ranged on the slopes to the south.

Back through the gate brings you to the purest example of Crusader architecture in Jerusalem: the **Church of St. Anne.** Saints Anne and Joachim, parents of the Virgin Mary, lived on this site when Mary was born, and you can visit the grotto beneath the church

On Mount of Olives' slope, the verdant Garden of Gethsemane.

where St. Anne gave birth. The church itself is plain and stocky. Built in Burgundian style, it was finished in 1140 during the reign of Fulk of Anjou, Crusader King of Jerusalem. Before that century was out. Jerusalem had been conquered by Moslems and the **35** church and convent became an Islamic seminary for a time. The buildings then crumbled until Napoleon III completely restored the church in the mid-19th century and presented it to the Order of the White Fathers (*Pères Blancs*).

Next to St. Anne's are excavations of the **Pool of Bethesda,** where sacrificial sheep were washed, and where Jesus cured the crippled man *(John 5:2–9)*. The lowest level of the pool dates from Hasmonean times; subsequently the Romans built a pagan shrine here, the Byzantines a large church to commemorate Jesus' miracle, and the Crusaders constructed a chapel, all swept away over the centuries – a real microcosm of Jerusalem's history.

After leaving the church rejoin the Via Dolorosa and walk up the street to the Franciscan monastery (the Convent of the Flagellation), starting-point for the walk along the Stations of the Cross.

Franciscan monks have been retracing Jesus' steps and caring for the holy sites along the Via Dolorosa since the 15th century. Walks are usually offered on Friday afternoons. Daily walking tours of the Old City, including portions of the Via Dolorosa, are organized by the Municipality and announced in the free tourist-office bulletin, *Events in the Jerusalem Region.* A small fee is charged. Or, licensed guides and neighbourhood boys will be glad to guide visitors; look for them near Station I, and settle on a fee in advance.

The Stations of the Cross

Some of the events mentioned in the Gospels can be matched with places along the Via Dolorosa, others are less sure, and a few are almost certainly the stuff of legends. In fact, today's 14 stations were mapped out in the 16th century by European Christians who had never been to Jerusalem, and who used documentary and hearsay evidence, which explains how the legendary stations crept in.

Pilgrims from Europe, who had read these descriptions, were not content to be shown only four or seven stations by Franciscan monks living in Jerusalem. The monks decided that faith could also be served by changing the plan of the stations to accommodate the pilgrims' pre-formed notions – thus Europeans' guesses became Jerusalem's "facts".

STATION I (Condemnation): Jesus was condemned in Herod's Antonia Fortress, the site of

Bearing the cross in Jesus' steps shows special devotion.

which is now covered by modern buildings. Tradition has it that Pilate delivered Jesus to his soldiers at a spot now in the courtyard of El-Omariye School, across the street from the Franciscan monastery.

STATION II (Jesus receives the cross): After being condemned, Jesus was taken away by the soldiers, who beat and mocked him in the fortress courtyard, put a crown of thorns on his head and led him away to be crucified *(Mark 15:16–20).* Much of the fortress courtyard pavement, made of huge flagstones, still exists in the monastery and the Convent of the Sisters of Zion, next door. You can see the pavement, or **Lithostrotos,** plus the Franciscans' Chapel of the Flagellation (a 37 mediaeval building that contains a Biblical museum) and the Chapel of Condemnation, which are both built upon the Lithostrotos.

Before being given the cross in the courtyard. Jesus was presented to the people by Pilate who said "Behold the man!" *(John 19:5)*. The site is likely to have been near the fortress entrance, or somewhat past the arch, built in A.D. 135, which is now named "Ecce Homo Arch".

STATION III (Jesus falls): The Gospels carry no word of this event, but tradition has it that

Spasm Armenian Catholic Church commemorates the meeting of Mary and Jesus.

STATION V (Simon carries Jesus' cross): In the Gospels, a man from Cyrenaica (Libya) was forced by the soldiers to carry the cross *(Matt. 27:32)* when it looked as though Jesus couldn't go on. A small 19th-century Franciscan oratory marks the spot.

STATION VI (Veronica wipes Jesus' face): Your guide will have a door in the wall opened, and you will step down into the little **Church of St. Veronica,** built in the restored vaults of a Crusader monastery. Tradition says a woman wiped the sweaty, bloody face of Jesus here, and an imprint was left on the cloth. The Latin for "True Image" has given us the name "Veronica", and since the woman's name is unknown she has become St. Veronica. The legend has been a part of Jerusalem lore since the 7th century and the mysterious cloth bearing the image is now kept at St. Peter's in Rome.

STATION VII (Jesus falls again): At the crossroads of the Via

Jesus fell under the weight of the cross just around the first corner you come to. A Polish chapel, with a relief showing Jesus bearing the cross, marks the spot.

STATION IV (Jesus meets his mother): A small shrine near the entrance to Our Lady of the

39

Dolorosa and the market street of Khan ez-Zeit is the spot where, tradition says, Jesus fell under the weight of the cross a second time.

STATION VII (Jesus speaks to Jerusalem's women): A cross in stone relief on the wall marks the site. St. Luke reports that Jesus stopped along the way to Golgotha and told the women who were following him that they should weep for themselves and their children rather than for him (*Luke 23:28*). In fact, a mere 36 years after Jesus' crucifixion, Jerusalem was destroyed by Roman troops, its citizens starved, killed in battle, executed or sold into slavery.

STATION IX (Jesus falls a third time): Jesus' third fall under the weight of the cross is legend, and therefore the exact location is disputed. Your guide will lead you south along Khan ez-Zeit from Station VIII, up a stairway to the **Ethiopian Convent** on the roof of the Church of the Holy Sepulchre. A bit of column embedded in a wall is now cited as Station IX, though it is of less interest than the convent itself. Stately Ethiopian monks occupy the curious rooftop settlement, the only part of the church which the Copts, one of the world's oldest Christian communities, can claim.

Holy Sepulchre Church shelters Golgotha and Jesus' tomb, most sacred spots in Christendom.

The Way of the Cross now leads into the **Church of the Holy Sepulchre** itself, which shelters the five final Stations. There has been a Church of the Holy Sepulchre on this spot for some 1,650 years, ever since Queen Helena visited Jerusalem and identified the site of Golgotha* in A.D. 326. Emperor Constantine the Great then had a magnificent basilica and rotunda built to house the tomb of Jesus. This, the grandest and richest of all churches to stand here, was destroyed in the year 614 by invading Persians. It was later rebuilt, but the form it has today dates mostly from Crusader times.

The plan of the church seems to have been drawn more by history than by a single architect, and bickering among clergy of various sects over rights within the church has added to the confusion. Disagreement was so bad

---

* The hill where Jesus was crucified was skull-shaped. The names "Golgotha" and "Calvary" derive from Hebrew and Latin words meaning "skull".

in the 19th century that the sultan had to step in and adjudicate the Christian dispute.

The portal by which visitors enter the church is from Crusader times (1149). The western door of the pair is open: the eastern door was bricked up a few years after the church's completion and has stayed that way ever since.

STATION X (Jesus is stripped): On stepping into the church, turn right and climb the narrow staircase. The platform here rests partly on the rock of Golgotha itself. The soldiers stripped Jesus of his clothes, which they later divided among themselves (Matt. 27:35), at this spot near the cross.

STATION XI (Jesus is nailed to the cross): The Franciscan chapel on the platform – the one to the right – is traditionally where Jesus was nailed to the cross.

STATION XII (Jesus' death): To the left of the Franciscan chapel is a Greek Orthodox altar, profusely decorated and attended by a black-robed priest. He will show you a hole under the altar, and a small silver disc marking the place where, tradition says, Jesus' cross was set up, with those of the two thieves on either side.

STATION XIII (Jesus is taken down from the cross): Between the Franciscan and Greek altars is a small shrine with an ancient wooden figure of Mary in a glass case. In the Gospels, Mary was present at Jesus' death (John 19:26).

Take the right-hand stairs down from the platform to the ground floor, and just in front of you will be the Stone of the Unction where Jesus' body was anointed with spices and myrrh and then interred a few steps away in Joseph of Arimathea's personal tomb.

STATION XIV (The Holy Sepulchre): Joseph of Arimathea, a follower of Jesus, donated the tomb, which was a two-room crypt cut in the rock of Golgotha. Most of the rock was cut away with the construction of earlier Churches of the Holy Sepulchre; all that remains is the stone shelf on which Jesus' body lay, now covered in polished marble. The present structure (aedicule) enclosing the tomb was designed by an Orthodox architect in the 19th century. The tiny chamber in which Jesus was buried can hold only six people at a time and you may have a few minutes' wait.

In the Church of the Holy Sepulchre itself there's plenty of room to move around. Over the

Station XIII: Mary wept as Jesus' body was removed from the cross.

centuries each corner and nook has taken on some significance, and small chapels have been dedicated to the different people and events related to Jesus' crucifixion and resurrection. Opposite the entrance to the aedicule is the **Greek Orthodox Katholikon,** a brilliantly decorated nave.

If you stand facing the aedicule with your back to the Katholikon, the Franciscan chapel of Mary Magdalene is on your right. This is the spot where, traditionally, Mary Magdalene discovered the resurrection of Jesus. A Franciscan convent, seminary and church are grouped around the chapel. **43**

Mount Zion

Directly south of the Old City, just outside the walls, is Mount Zion. Few places in the world can claim equal significance with this barren Judean hilltop, revered by millions and visited by hundreds daily. Leaving the Old City, you pass through Zion Gate which is pitted with bullet holes from the modern wars which have raged around it. For a good look at Mount Zion, the Old City, and surrounding Judean hills, take a walk along the top of the walls near Zion Gate. Stairways and railings just inside the gate make it safe.

Mount Zion is dominated by the **Dormition Abbey** of the Benedictine monks. Coming from Zion Gate, bear right to reach the entrance, but note that no visits are allowed between noon and 2 p.m. Less than a century old, the abbey is a mixture of ancient styles and modern construction. The sanctuary has beautiful gold and polychrome mosaics in the Byzantine style, but the abbey's

Dormition Abbey is Mount Zion's Romanesque crown. Legend says Mary went to heaven from here.

spiritual centre is beneath the sanctuary, in the crypt. An effigy of the Virgin Mary marks the spot where she is said to have spent her last days on earth before her assumption into heaven.

On the opposite side of the Dormition Abbey from its entrance are two more sites of great religious significance. In a tiny low-ceiling room in one of the buildings is the **Tomb of King David.** A guard will provide men with head-coverings, in order to visit. Directly above the tomb, in the same building, is the **Coenaculum** ("dining room") believed to be the place where Jesus and his disciples shared the Last Supper, in celebration of the first night of Passover. The Crusaders built the Gothic archwork, and Turkish rulers of Jerusalem added a prayer niche and inscriptions. It's a small and humble room, hardly the grand hall of Leonardo da Vinci's famous painting.

Before you leave Mount Zion, visit the **Chamber of the Martyrs,** beneath the other buildings on the Mount, which commemorates the sacrifice of millions of Jewish lives in the Nazi holocaust. The plaques on the walls give the names of the communities which were destroyed.

Mount of Olives

The best way to visit the Mount of Olives is to take a bus (No. 75 to Et-Tur, from the East Jerusalem bus station) or taxi to the top of the Mount, visit the points of interest there, and then walk down the hillside through the Jewish cemeteries and the Garden of Gethsemane to the Kidron Valley.

Driving through the valley called Wadi el-Guz or Nahal Egoz and up the slopes of the Mount of Olives takes you past the Augusta Victoria Hospital, and, after turning at the crest of the hill, the Greek church of Viri Galilei ("Men of Galilee") is on the right. Farther along is the imposing tower of the Russian Church of the Ascension. The tower's top is the highest point in the city and appropriately it marks the spot from which, according to Orthodox Russian belief, Jesus ascended to heaven. The nuns in the convent here preserve their seclusion, and visitors must have special permission.

Most other Christian denominations accept the **Chapel of the Ascension** as the place of Jesus' ascension. Down the road from the Russian church, the dome is now in the grounds of a little mosque. The modest structure is built over a rock said to be the last upon which Jesus stood. Don't expect a architectural masterpiece when you visit the chapel; despite its significance, it's very plain.

Near the Chapel of the Ascension you'll find relief for weary feet. Several camel-drivers always wait around the mosque entrance and will be glad to order their huge beasts to kneel down so that you can climb on easily. Depending on how much you're prepared to pay, they will trot you down to the 7-Arches Hotel, or just wait while you have your photo taken.

Just south of the chapel is the **Pater Noster Church**, thought to be built on the spot where Jesus taught his disciples the Lord's Prayer. The present church dates from the late 19th century. Inside, wall decorations include the Lord's Prayer in dozens of languages. In the same compound you'll find the Basilica of Eleona, finished in 1923 on the site of a Byzantine church.

From the Pater Noster church compound, a road heads to Bethphage, traditional starting-point for Jesus' triumphal ride into Jerusalem on the first Palm Sunday. Some ancient Jewish tombs

nearly help to conjure up a vivid picture of what the area looked like two thousand years ago.

A short distance along the main road from Pater Noster Church is the 7-Arches Hotel, and in front of it an observation point for the breathtaking **view** of Old Jerusalem. A small amphitheatre provides a convenient observation point. Looking across the Kidron Valley, one's eye is immediately drawn to the sheen of the golden Dome of the Rock and its brilliantly coloured tiles. The eastern city wall, with a Moslem graveyard at its foot, is broken by the impressive grace of the **Golden Gate** (also called Mercy Gate or Eternal Gate). The gate has been walled in for centuries, and many believe it will not be reopened until the Messiah appears and enters Jerusalem. The Byzantines built the splendid gate on the ruins of earlier ones; the Crusaders added and embellished it in the 12th century, and Sultan Suleiman repaired it in the 16th. The Lions' (St. Stephen's) Gate is to the right of Golden Gate.

Scanning the ancient and sacred city from the Mount of Olives, it's easy to see why so many devout people of different religions regard Mount Zion as the place where the Messiah will make his presence known. Looking from north to south, the hill stands out at the far end, crowned by the conical roof of the Dormition Abbey. This sweeping vista of Jerusalem has changed greatly over the centuries, but has never failed to stir the souls of the countless pilgrims who have made the long journey to the Holy Land.

North along the road from the observation point, a narrow road descends into the extensive Jewish cemeteries on the slope, the oldest and largest in the world. Some graves go back to biblical times. The pebbles placed on top symbolize a visit by a devoted mourner. Just off the downward road are the **Tombs of the Prophets,** sombre rock-hewn tunnels carved with burial niches said to contain the remains of Zechariah, Haggai, Malachi and many others.

On the way down the hill, the 19th-century church of **Dominus Flevit** ("The Lord Wept") commemorates Jesus' weeping over Jerusalem (*Luke 19: 41–42*). During construction, artefacts, tombs and ruins from Jerusalem's history were uncovered, some dating from late Bronze Age times (about 1600 B.C.).

The **Garden of Gethsemane** occupies the lower part of the slope, and various plots are cared for by different sects. The **Russian Orthodox Church** of Mary Magdalene with its gilded onion-shaped domes is in the first area of the garden. The exquisite church was built by order of Tsar Alexander III and his brothers in memory of their mother. Entering the church's one large room, your eye is immediately caught by the marvellously smooth and lustrous white marble of the iconostasis. The body of the Russian Grand Duchess Elizabeth reposes in the church's crypt. Russian Orthodox nuns oversee the church and its grounds.

On the lower reaches of the slope of the Mount of Olives, leading on to the Jericho Road, is the **Basilica of the Agony,** also called the Church of All Nations, the tympanum of its façade shining with brilliant mosaic work. In the mosaic scene, Christ weeps as he prays in Gethsemane (*Luke 22: 41–45*). The church was built on the site of Byzantine and Crusader ruins, paid for by donations from people all over the world, and dedicated by the Franciscans in 1924. Glass plates in the church floor allow you to see fragments **47** of the Byzantine floor mosaics left from the earlier church.

The highlight of a visit to the Basilica is a walk in the garden, which harbours some gnarled and venerable olive trees. They say an olive tree never dies but sprouts new wood when an old trunk is decrepit: these ancient trees may have been there when Jesus walked in the garden. "Gethsemane" comes from the Hebrew *Geth-shemma*, meaning "oilpress".

A few steps from the Basilica of the Agony, at the head of the Kidron Valley, is **Mary's Tomb.** Through an attractive Crusader arch, stairs lead down a long and dingy passageway to the Orthodox Church of the Assumption. In the gloomy subterranean church is a rock-hewn sepulchre. Hundreds of smoky, scented votive lamps hang from the ceiling. Some traditions give this as the place of Mary's burial and assumption into heaven, though the Dormition Abbey on Mount Zion also claims the honour.

The Franciscan **Grotto of Gethsemane,** entered by turning right before reaching the Crusader arch, is a less sombre place. Jesus may well have gathered here with his disciples during the

years of his teaching; visits are during slightly shorter hours than at the Basilica of the Agony.

In Jerusalem, every stone and structure has its significance. The little Moslem shrine by the road near Mary's Tomb is the grave of

Jesus may well have knelt beneath this ancient Gethsemane olive tree.

15th-century Moslem judge and historian, Mujr ed-Din. Nearby, at the head of the Kidron Valley, the Greek Orthodox Church of St. Stephen commemorates the first Christian martyr (*Acts 7: 59–60*). Up the Jericho Road toward the city is a small but dramatic monument to Israeli soldiers killed in the 1967 Six-Day War.

The Kidron Valley

(Valley of Jehoshaphat)

The valley between Temple Mount and the Mount of Olives holds traces left by its earliest inhabitants. The original settlement of Jerusalem, founded perhaps around 3000 B.C., was on the western side of this valley, and tombs and monuments have been built here ever since.

Gravestones with crosses and Arabic inscriptions at the head of the valley remind foreign visitors that many Arabs are Christians. Most of the graves are recent, barely a century old, but the striking, timeworn monument seen down the valley is thought to date from the Second Temple period over two thousand years ago. Legend says it is the **Tomb of Absalom.** Behind it is the smaller Tomb of Jehoshaphat, dating from the same period.

Though many legends are connected with the set of tombs farther on, an inscription sets us right. The Tomb of Bnei Hezir was carved in Greek style from the rock of the valley wall for a Jewish priestly family (the Sons of Hezir) of the 2nd century B.C. Whether or not St. James ever took refuge or was buried here, as Christian tradition says, we may never know for certain.

A four-sided pyramid tops the **Tomb of Zechariah,** dating from about the time of Jesus. No one is sure who is buried here: Zechariah the prophet (who is also said to be interred in the Tombs of the Prophets, up the hill), or Zechariah the father of John the Baptist.

Gazing up to the south-eastern corner of the city walls, you are actually looking at the site of King David's city, which would have been a tiny village by today's standards. It occupied the slope of the hill south of El-Aksa Mosque, called the Ophel, or **City of David,** open to the public as an archaeological park. Modern excavations have brought to light the support wall of David's citadel (itself vanished) and the upper end of a tunnel which led to Gihon Spring. (The lower part was discovered a century ago.) The settlement was situated here partly because of the spring in a cavern just to the west of the modern road. It lay outside the city walls in ancient times, and is the same source for which the

Zechariah's Tomb is cloaked in mystery; above are smaller tombs.

50

Jebusites constructed an earlier tunnel (see p. 12).

Visitors are free to wander the hillside and explore the tunnel. A small museum displays photographs and models of Jerusalem's water system. Soon to go on view in the park are reconstructed houses from various periods, including Canaanite dwellings built 5,000 years ago.

In 701 B.C., King Hezekiah had another tunnel dug, to the **Pool of Siloam,** which was within the city walls southwest of the Gihon. Under siege by the ferocious Assyrians, the king and his people quaffed the cool water of Gihon while the Assyrians sat with parched throats. Long afterwards, legend says that the Virgin Mary brought her infant son's clothes here to wash them. The Pool of Siloam, moreover, has its own reputation as the place where Jesus restored sight to a blind man *(John 9:6–7)*. A church was once built over this spot, but today the minaret of a small mosque is the best landmark for finding the pool.

The lower reaches of the Kidron Valley are now filled by the Arab town of SILWAN. The town tumbles down the southern end of the Mount of Olives, known here as the "Mount of Offence", having acquired a disreputable name in the time of Solomon. The great king built altars to pagan gods worshipped by his non-Jewish wives on this slope, a terrible offence against the God of Israel *(1 Kings 11:1–12)*. Today nothing remains of those ill-founded altars.

East Jerusalem

Though Jerusalem was reunited after the Six-Day War in 1967, the parts earlier held by Jordan retain their Arab way of life. East Jerusalem has its modern streets and ancient monuments just as West Jerusalem does, and because East and West were separate cities in earlier years, you will find a Central Post Office, bus station, YMCA, and even consulates duplicated in both parts of the city. The Arabs of East Jerusalem, whether Christian or Moslems, warmly welcome foreign visitors of all religions as they have for centuries.

If you are not staying in one of East Jerusalem's hotels, spend at least one morning in this part of the city, perhaps with a return in the evening for an Arabic dinner

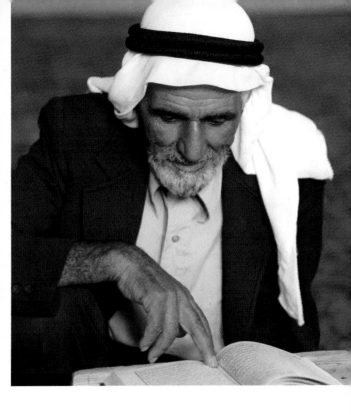

and an oriental show. Remember the Sabbath difference: the Moslem Arabs have Friday as their day of rest, from sunset on Thursday to sunset on Friday. Shops are closed, though restaurants are open all week.

The preoccupation of many Jerusalem citizens: thoughtful study.

A good place to begin your wanderings is Damascus Gate. Walk north on the Nablus Road **53**

CENTRAL JERUSALEM

(Derech Shechem) and look for a lane on the right with a sign pointing to the **Garden Tomb.** General Gordon, British hero of China and Khartoum, visited Jerusalem in 1883 and found that this rock-hewn cave fitted very well the description of Jesus' tomb. A skull-like hill is close by, and a vision strengthened Gordon's belief in its authenticity. An association of British Protestants owns and maintains the attractive grounds and gardens, and welcomes all visitors. Whether this is Jesus' burial-place or not, the tomb is "unspoiled" compared to the one in the Church of the Holy Sepulchre.

At the intersection of the Nablus Road and Saladin Street, you are in the American Colony, named after the late 19th-century benefactors who started a suburb here as Jerusalem emerged from the ancient city walls. The imposing church tower is that of St. George's Anglican Cathedral, seat of the Anglican Archbishop of Jerusalem and of a school and seminary. You may stroll into the "close" if the gates are open.

Just east of the intersection, in Saladin Street, is the entrance to the eerie **Tombs of the Kings,** actually the 1st-century B.C. tomb of Queen Helena of Adiab-ne, in Mesopotamia. As you descend the staircase, a guide from the caretaker's family may catch up with you and point out the tomb's curiosities: grooves cut in the rock to catch rainwater and convey it to cisterns, the rolling stone door which sealed the tomb, and the burial niches. At the end of the tour your guide will politely request a tip many times greater than he expects to receive.

The Nablus Road takes you past the American Colony Hotel, once the palace of a Turkish pasha, to the small Sheikh Jarrah Mosque which gives this part of the city its name. Past the mosque, turn right, and then left, to reach the **Tomb of Simon the Just** (Shimeon Hazadik), a high priest during the Second Temple period. Orthodox Jews hold the site sacred, though an inscription attrib-

Sepulchres like the Garden Tomb were common during Jesus' time.

utes the grave to a Roman owner. As this is Jerusalem, both accounts of the ownership may be true.

North-east of Simon's Tomb rises **Mount Scopus**. From 1948 to 1967 this was an Israeli enclave within East Jerusalem. The Hebrew University and the Hadassah **57**

Medical Centre were active here before 1948, closed during partition, and are again in operation today. The Harry Truman Research Institute is the most striking of the new buildings. The university library serves as Israel's National Library. You'll need to go by car, taxi or bus to reach the heights of the Mount.

Admire the view of the Judean **58** hills and desert from the **amphi-** **theatre** built into the hillside, or come for an open-air concert here on a summer's evening.

On your return to the centre of East Jerusalem from Mount Scopus, you will pass the British War Cemetery for the soldiers who fell fighting for Jerusalem in 1917 – another reminder of the city's turbulent history. You can make a diversion to the **Tombs of the Sanhedrin,** the supreme rabbinical court of Second Temple times. The impressive rock-hewn tombs are in the Sanhedria quarter.

Retracing your steps from Simon's Tomb to St. George's, take Saladin Street to explore the central area of East Jerusalem's modern business district, perhaps stopping for a *kayek* (pronounced KAH-yek, from the English "cake"), an oval-shaped bread roll sprinkled with sesame seeds.

Traditional life-styles are the soul of Jerusalem (Mount Scopus).

At the end of Saladin Street are the city walls and Herod's Gate, part of Sultan Suleiman's construction, though resting on even more ancient foundations. Herod's Gate remained closed for centuries, but was reopened in 1875 as the city expanded. **59**

Across Sultan Suleiman Street from Herod's Gate is the **Rockefeller Museum** (see p. 87) perched on a hill. John D. Rockefeller Jr. gave the money to build the museum in 1927. The plot of land chosen as the site gives it a lofty position – right in the path of hundreds of bullets during the 1967 war, as you'll notice by the pitted surface of its stone exterior.

Two more curiosities exist in this area, both underground. Find the bus station on Sultan Suleiman Street between Nablus Road and Saladin Street. A narrow alley runs along the eastern edge of the station to a rocky outcrop. Within the outcrop – which is actually the "Skull Hill" of the Garden Tomb – is a cave called Jeremiah's Grotto, from a tradition that the Prophet Jeremiah wrote the Book of Lamentations here and was then laid to rest.

On the opposite side of Sultan Suleiman Street, signs direct visitors to a garden and the entrance to **Solomon's Quarries,** from which the stone used to build Second Temple Jerusalem was cut. This cavern is also known as "Zedekiah's Cave", from a story that King Zedekiah and his army escaped from a siege of Jerusalem in 587 B.C. via this route.

West Jerusalem

West of Damascus Gate and the Nablus Road is the Jerusalem which is the capital city of Israel. The Knesset – the Israeli parliament – and the ministries and government offices are spread over the hilltops outside the business and residential section of Jerusalem. You can easily tour the centre of modern Jerusalem on foot; to reach the sights of the outlying districts you have a choice between city buses and taxis.

Starting-point for a walk in West Jerusalem is **Zahal Square,** at the westernmost corner of the Old City walls. In the late 19th century, the growth of modern Jerusalem was so great that the Ottoman monarch, Sultan Abdul Hamid II, decided to open a new gate in the city walls to serve the new colonies to the west. The result was New Gate (1887), a few steps north-east of the square.

Just across the street from New Gate is the enormous hospice and monastery of Notre Dame of Jerusalem, built in the same year as New Gate. Once administered by the Augustinian Fathers of the Assumption, it is now a hostel for pilgrims.

Across Jaffa Road from the Central Post Office are buildings now housing the Law Courts, but which were at one time part of the **Russian Compound**, a walled area built at the end of the 1800s to house, feed and care for 10,000 Russian pilgrims all at once. Turn right after passing the Law Courts for a look at the compound's huge, green-domed church.

Continuing north-east on Jaffa Road soon brings you to **Zion Square** in the heart of West Jerusalem's centre. From the square you can continue along Jaffa Road to reach the colourful marketplace of **Makhane Yehuda,**

As a young sabra (child born in Israel), you're at the centre of world affairs. West Jerusalem's cafes are alive with political talk.

Mea She'arim

Since the times of the biblical Pharisees many groups of Orthodox Jews have tried to rigorously observe the tenets of Hebrew religious law. The quarter called Mea She'arim, north of Zion Square, is the home of Orthodox communities which live the strictly religious life. Signs warn visitors to dress modestly – women must have heads and shoulders covered and wear longish skirts (no trousers), and men should have head coverings. The Sabbath brings a halt to all work here, even the driving of cars, as families flock to the many small synagogues which preserve traditions from around the world. Though you are free to wander through Mea She'arim as you wish, be careful to observe the customs of the quarter and you will find the residents friendly and helpful. The best way to visit the synagogues is to sign up for the excellent **synagogue tour** arranged by one of the city's travel agencies. If you visit during the Day of Rejoicing of the Torah, don't miss the celebration in Mea She'arim.

In Mea She'arim, life is lived to the letter of biblical law; religious duties are foremost.

especially crowded before the Sabbath and holidays. Fresh fruit and vegetables are piled high, and hunks of meat displayed; the air is filled with the scent of oriental spices, and the vendors announce their wares in a loud chant. Continuing along Jaffa Road, Jerusalem's Central Bus Station has services to all parts of the city and country. You'll find Binyanei Ha'oomah, Jerusalem's convention and exhibition centre capable of accommodating some 3,500 people, in this area.

Another direction to take from Zion Square is up **Ben Yehuda**, a pedestrian road lined with shops and open-air cafés. The area becomes liveliest around sunset, with folk-singers, portrait artists, jewellery salesmen and other diversions. Nearby is the newly renovated **Nachlat Shiv'a**, a centre for pubs and restaurants.

At the top of Ben Yehuda Street, turn left into King George V Street. Farther down is the semi-circular headquarters of the Jewish Agency. Keren Hayesod (United Israel Appeal) and Keren Kayemet (Jewish National Fund) also have offices here. Just past the Jewish Agency compound, at the corner of Agron, Ramban and

Aza Streets, rises the bold and massive façade of **Hekhal Shlomo,** seat of the chief Rabbis, both Sephardic and Ashkenazi, of Israel. You can enter to see museum exhibits of ceremonial objects, biblical dioramas, and the complete interior of an 18th-century Paduan synagogue.

On the other side of King George V Street is Jerusalem's **Independence Park.** The Mamilla Pool, near a small Moslem cemetery at the eastern end of the park, is thought to be part of the Old City's ancient water system. Wander through the refreshing greenery of the park to the intersection of Agron, King David and Mamilla Streets, and climb the hill along King David Street past the modern campus of Hebrew Union College. Soon the oriental tower of the **YMCA** will loom above your head on the right. This landmark was built in 1933, and contains the city's first swimming pool. The **view** over Jerusalem from the top of the building's 150-foot tower is magnificent.

The imposing bulk of the **King David Hotel** (1930) is across the street from the YMCA. It was the city's first grand hotel. The entire south wing was blown up by bombs in 1946 when the hotel was used as a gathering-place for British Protectorate personnel; 91 people died in the attack by the Irgun movement. Reconstructed, the hotel still serves VIPs.

At Plumer Square, you are at the centre of a district of fine gardens. Make your way to that curious and completely unexpected structure looming a short distance away: a true-to-life stone **windmill.** The mill and the quarter around it were built in the mid-1800s through the initiative of Jewish Jerusalem's greatest 19th-century patron, Sir Moses Montefiore. The English philanthropist visited the city several times, and organized the construction of Mishkenot Shaananim, a row of dwellings built to encourage Jews to move from dilapidated houses within the walls to more modern and healthy places. Near to Mishkenot Shaananim you'll find the **Yemin Moshe Quarter:** it's not only architecturally captivating, but also harbours several interesting artists' studios and galleries.

Israeli soldiers face danger daily as they patrol the city; but off duty the job has its moments.

Farther Out

Farther west from Zion Square, but still accessible by city bus (No. 9), are many more points of interest. The **Knesset,** Israel's parliament, meets in an attractive modern building on a hilltop and you can tour the legislators' domain. Bring your passport or identity card. As you alight from the bus, look first at the attractive giant **menorah** (seven-branched candelabrum) opposite the Knesset entrance, a present from the Mother of Parliaments.

Amid the modern and often daring architecture of this area is the ancient **Greek Monastery of the Cross,** over a thousand years old. If we can believe the legends, the trees which once grew here were planted by Lot after he fled Sodom, and one of them was later used to fashion Jesus' cross.

Spread along the hillside above the Monastery of the Cross are the pavillions of the great **Israel Museum,** actually four museums in one (see p. 85). On the next hilltop to the west is the Hebrew University's new campus (1954), a sprawling collection of buildings constructed after the original campus on Mount Scopus was surrounded in 1948.

Even farther west are several impressive monuments to 20th-century people and events that changed the world. **Mount Herzl** is named after the Austro-Hungarian writer and founder of Zionism whose work aided the eventual establishment of the State of Israel (see p. 18). Herzl's tomb is here, plus a small museum, and in the attractive gardens nearby lie other modern Israeli leaders, including Prime Ministers Levi Eshkol and Golda Meir.

Not far from Mount Herzl is **Yad Vashem** on the Mount of Remembrance, dedicated to the memory of the millions of Jews murdered by the Nazis. Memorials, a documentation centre and a terrifying but effective exhibit showing the horrors of Nazism fill the hilltop and fascinate visitors, who leave Yad Vashem saddened but somehow strengthened.

After Mount Herzl the road divides; the upper branch goes to Hadassah Medical Centre, the lower to the village of **Ein Kerem,** lying in the hills surrounded by olive trees and vineyards. Ein Kerem is thought to be the birthplace of John the Baptist, where Mary visited her cousin Elizabeth. Two Franciscan churches built over Crusader and Byzantine ruins

Memorial to concentration camp victims reminds and pleads: never again.

are said to be the sites of these events. Ein Kerem is named after a spring also called Mary's Fountain. There are Russian and Greek Orthodox convents in the village.

The upper road to **Hadassah Medical Centre** has several names, but near the hospital it becomes the Street of Henrietta Szold, named after the founder of

Hadassah, the Organization of American Women Zionists. Marc Chagall designed the **windows** in the hospital's small synagogue, and many visitors come to admire the designs of the dozen windows, each signifying one of the twelve tribes. Audiovisual shows are presented in the hospital complex.

On a side road are two memorials – the **Kennedy Memorial**, like a tree stump, representing a life cut off in its prime, and a piano keyboard motif honouring Arthur Rubenstein. Another road south from Mount Herzl leads to a popular model of ancient Jerusalem in the grounds of the Holyland Hotel.

Twentieth-century tributes: swirling colours of brilliant windows by Marc Chagall, and the impressively restrained Kennedy Memorial.

Excursions

On the Road to the Desert

On the way to the biblical town of Bethlehem from East Jerusalem, stop for a look at the Tomb of Rachel. Revered by Jews, Christians and Moslems alike, this famous mother is sought out by women who come to this simple tomb to pray for fertility. The small domed monument over the tomb dates from the 15th century.

A security note: unless you are with a tour group, it's sensible to ask about the latest situation before setting out for Bethlehem, the West Bank and other areas.

Bethlehem's church towers and minarets are spread dramatically along the Judean hilltops. The population, mostly Arab, is divided between Christians and Moslems. Manger Square, busy with taxis and buses, is in front of the **Church of the Nativity.** One of the oldest in the world, it has seen many changes since Constantine had it built in 325. You enter through a small, low door, designed to keep potential aggressors from riding in. The church is situated above the Grotto of the

Nativity, a small subterranean chamber in which a silver star marks the place of Jesus' birth. A side chapel is said to be where the manger stood. The Church of the Nativity, like the Church of the Holy Sepulchre, is divided into zones of possession among Christian sects, but the visitor is free to wander from one to another.

On the road south towards Hebron, you will see a strange

conical hill, off to the east. This is the **Herodium,** a stupendous 300-foot-high artificial mountain built by Herod the Great and once topped with lavish palaces, and defensive towers and battlements. Herod was later buried here.

The road from Bethlehem to Hebron passes Solomon's Pools, three reservoirs that helped supply Jerusalem, some 13 kilometres away, with water via an aqueduct.

Candles have steadily burned in the Church of the Nativity for over sixteen hundred years.

The terraced hillsides are covered with Hebron's famous vineyards. This has been a winemaking region since Noah's time. To the east is the wilderness of Judea.

The town of **Hebron**, 20 miles south of Jerusalem, stands at 3,000 feet above sea level, and its great age is attested to by the Cave of Makhpelah, containing the **Tombs of the Patriarchs.** In the centre of town, now covered by a mosque, lie the remains of Abraham, Issac and Jacob, and of their wives Sarah, Rebecca and Leah. The tombs are in the cave within the building's Herodian foundations. "Memorial tombs" – not containing remains – are centres for devotions by Jews, Christians and Moslems. The **mosque,** once a Crusader church, has beautiful Mameluke stone and mosaics, some of the finest Islamic decoration in Israel. A side chapel, or "Women's Mosque", is said to contain the tomb of Joseph, who was sold into slavery by his brothers. There are different times for Moslems and non-Moslems to visit the mosque above the tombs.

Some 45 kilometres south of Hebron, on the edge of the desert, is **Beersheba** (Well of the Oath). About 4,000 years ago Abraham dug a well here, but it was not until 1948 that the town sprang to life. Today, Beersheba has over 128,000 inhabitants, many of them new immigrants who have come to help make the desert bloom and reap its natural wealth.

Be sure to stay at Beersheba on a Wednesday night so you can get up early on Thursday morning for the picturesque **camel market,** which starts at 6 a.m. By 9 a.m. the camel and goat selling ends, but Bedouin handicrafts, such as copperware, jewellery, embroidered camel bags and handwoven rugs, are for sale until about 2 p.m.

Things to see and do in Beersheba reflect the city's character as "Capital of the Negev". Catch up on the history of the city and the desert at the **museum,** housed in a disused Turkish mosque (built in 1915) set in its own little park. **Abraham's Well** can still be seen down the hill at the southern end of Keren Kayemet Le-Israel Street, probably reconstructed many times over the centuries.

To the Dead Sea

The old road from Jerusalem to Jericho passes around the Mount of Olives and then through the Arab town of El-Azariye, or **Bethany.** The Arab name comes from Azar, or Lazarus, for his tomb is to the left off the road and up the hill. In Bethany Jesus called Lazarus forth from the tomb *(John 11: 41–44)*, making this a happy rather than sombre

EXCURSIONS

10   20   30 km

10   20 miles

MEDITERRANEAN

N

LEBANON

Metulla
Kiryat Shmona
El Quneitra
Rosh Hanikra
Ma'alot
Tarshiha
Zefat (Safad)
Nahariyya
Mt. of Beatitudes
Capernaum
Acre (Akko)
Karmiel
Tabgha
Sea of Galilee
HAIFA
Kiryat Ata
Tiberias
Mt. Carmel
Kiryat Tiv'on
NAZARETH
Yoq'ne'am
Zikhron Ya'aqov
Afula
Caesarea
Megiddo
Bet She'an
Jenin
Hadera
Jordan
Netanya
Tulkarm
Tubas
SAMARIA
Nablus
Herzliyya
Petakh Tikva
Abud
TEL AVIV-JAFFA (YAFO)
Taiyiba
AMMAN
Bat Yam
Lod
Ramla
Ramallah
Rehovot
Jericho
Ashdod
JERUSALEM
Bet Shemesh
Bethany
Qumran
Bethlehem
Ashkelon
J U D E A
Kiryat Gat
Gaza
Lakhish
Dura
HEBRON
Sa'ad
Ein Gedi
Bet Qama
Yatta
Netivot
Dead Sea
-390
Ma'on
M O A B
Masada
Arad
BEERSHEBA
ISMA'ILIYA   EILAT, AQABA

GALILEE

SYRIA

JORDAN

sepulchre. A Crusader fortress-convent and a modern Franciscan church are near the tomb.

Until 1967 there were only a few Bedouin tents on the road from Jerusalem to Jericho. Today you pass the fast-growing town of Ma'aleh Adumim. Between the

hills, clusters of trees and red-tiled houses mark new villages. After Ma'aleh Adumim, you pass the site of **The Good Samaritan**. A little further on, a side-road and footpath lead to the Greek Orthodox **Monastery of St. George**, built into the cliffside of the gorge of Wadi Kelt. The remote monastery once catered to hundreds of monks. Today, only a handful live here, remaining true to the timeless disciplines of simple living and prayer.

Moses first gazed on the Promised Land from a hill opposite **Jericho,** said to be the oldest city in the world, and the first to be conquered by the Israelites led by Joshua *(Josh. 6:1–21)*. People still come today wanting to see the famous "walls of Jericho". forgetting that they came tumbling down long ago. A great mound of rubble now marks the spot where the ancient city was built. Nearby, the Mount of Temptation is said to be the place where Jesus was tempted by Satan *(Matt. 4:8–11)*.

The highway junction just south of Jericho is where you join the road to **Qumran.** The Dead Sea Scrolls (see p. 87) were discovered in this area, once occupied by a Jewish sect called the

Essenes who spent their time farming, studying the holy law and trying to live the moral life. Ruins of their settlement are clearly marked for easy touring.

The road goes through the popular Dead Sea resort of **Ein Gedi,** a good place for lunch, a swim or a walk on the nature trails.

Even farther south along the Dead Sea, you come to **Masada.** As you approach it, you can see that this one flat-topped mountain stands apart from the others, making it perfect for a fortress. It was at Masada that the last group of Jewish Zealots held out in the

No hands! In the mineral-saturated Dead Sea, even non-swimmers easily stay afloat.

rebellion against Rome. By A.D. 73 the Romans had held the mountain in siege for three years. Knowing the Romans to be about to use a mighty ramp, the Jewish defenders committed mass suicide rather than give the Romans the triumph of capturing them.

An inn, youth hostel, snack bar and kosher restaurant are at the foot of the mountain near the cable car station. If you decide to 75 climb to the 1,450-foot high summit*, the Snake Path facing the Dead Sea is long and hard (an hour or so for the climb up), but the Bank Path on the western side of the mountain is much easier. Start your climb early, for it's very hot here even in spring and autumn. Even if you take the cable car, drink much more liquid than normal. Dehydration and sunstroke are common here.

At the top of Masada, cisterns provide drinking water and signs mark the sites of important structures. Even with the well-stocked granaries and reservoirs kept by the defenders here, it still seems miraculous that they could have held out for three years against the vastly superior forces of the Roman legions.

* As a result of the low altitude of the region, the summit is actually only about 135 feet above sea level.

Sea of Galilee

Whether you stop for a swim or not, don't miss a meal of fresh lakefish at **Tiberias** (Tveriya), an old and pretty town (now one of Israel's most popular seaside resorts) on the shore of Lake Kinneret, the Sea of Galilee. After the destruction of Jerusalem in A.D. 70, Tiberias became a centre for rabbinic study: the Mishnah (part of the Talmud) was finished here, and the Hebrew alphabet refined; Maimonides, one of Judaism's greatest religious philosophers, is buried in Tiberias. Born in Islamic-ruled Spain in 1135, this expert in Jewish law was also private physician to the sultan Saladin.

At TABGHA, north of Tiberias, is the Church of the Multiplication,

Masada: Zealots in unbelievable privation held off Rome's army.

where Jesus fed the multitudes with only a few loaves and fishes *(Matt. 14:19–20)*. Four kilometres from Tabgha, on the road to Capernaum, a glance at the small Mount of Beatitudes shows why Jesus chose it as the place for the Sermon on the Mount *(Matt. 5, 6, 7)*: the small hill is a perfect natural pulpit.

Jesus chose his first disciples from among the fishermen of **Capernaum** (Kefar-Nahum), and the foundations of a house here are said to be those of Simon Peter's. But Capernaum's most important ruins are those of a large and rich **synagogue** in the Roman style, built soon after Jerusalem's destruction. Simon Peter's house and the synagogue are next door to one another.

Also in Galilee, halfway between Tiberias and Haifa, is **Nazareth,** the town where Jesus grew up. Today, the population is almost evenly divided among Jews, Christians and Moslems. The **Church of the Annunciation** is a tremendous modern monument built for the Franciscans in the 1960s. It is constructed over the grotto where Mary received the news that she would bear a son and should call him **78** Jesus *(Luke 1:28–35)*.

Haifa and Environs

The third largest city in Israel, **Haifa** is known for both its industry and scenic beauty. It is dominated by the verdant heights of Mount Carmel ("God's Vineyard"), mentioned several times in the Bible for its beauty. After many centuries of colourful history, which included Crusader conquest, the city was destroyed in the 18th century. Its rebirth came in the 19th as European immigrants began to arrive, and started to plan the new Haifa, which Theodor Herzl had predicted would be the "city of the future". The builders' success is evident, as despite the ships, factories and trade centres Haifa is full of parks and beaches, tree-lined streets and sweeping vistas.

A cable car runs from the sea up to the heights of **Mount Carmel**, by the Carmelite church of Stella Maris. This is designated as the place where the miracle-prone prophet Elijah, helped by anti-idolatry Israelite forces, slew the pagan priests. There are several attractive residential quarters, and also Rehov Yefe Nof, the aptly named "Panorama Road", from which you may scan the whole city and its port.

Higher up are Haifa University and the Technion (technological institute), where "sight and sound" shows highlight technological advances. Just below Panorama Road are the Persian Gardens which surround the Baha'i Shrine, restingplace of Mirza Ali Muhammad, the 19th-century visionary. He was known to his followers as the "Gate of Faith" (Bab ed-Din) through whose leadership they would be able to enter paradise.

Down the slopes of Mount Carmel is the centre of modern Haifa, the business area called Hadar Ha'Carmel. Herzl Street is its lifeline, with shops and various services including a tourist information office. But the highlight of Haifa for many is **Elija's Cave,** at the foot of the mount, which sheltered the prophet when he fled from the king of Israel.

DALIYAT EL KARMIL, 22 kilometres south-east of Haifa, will introduce you to the daily life of the Druze people, whose Moslem-inspired religious beliefs are kept secret. EIN HOD, 12 kilometres south of Haifa, is a former Arab village that has become famous as an artists' colony.

Caesarea, almost exactly half-way between Haifa and Tel Aviv, was built in about 20 B.C. by Herod the Great and named after the emperor Caesar Augustus. The city's history is a gory one. In A.D. 66 it was the site of a Jewish uprising against the Romans; in 1101 it was taken by the Crusaders; in 1187 by Saladin, and in 1191 by Richard the Lion-Heart, among others, only to be destroyed by Mamelukes the following century. Thereafter it was left in peace and ruins.

With its ancient walls and gates, bridges, towers and fortifications, the **Crusader city** is worth visiting. Other impressive ruins near the city include the 2nd-century **Roman amphitheatre** (site of summer concerts and theatre) and **aqueduct.**

Today, the town is essentially a holiday centre, providing sandy beaches, sailing boats and sun.

North of Haifa is **Acre** (Akko), capital city of the region from Phoenician times until early in the present century. Similar to Caesarea's storybook history, Acre's past included visits by Caesar and Saladin, the Knights of St. John, Richard the Lion-Heart and Napoleon Bonaparte who laid siege to the town in 1799 but eventually had to retreat. You can still see much evidence from this romantic past within the medieval walls of the Old City. The **Mosque of El Jezzar** is the city's most impressive, built in 1781 by the ferocious Turkish governor, Ahmed Jezzar Pasha. Next to it is the **Hammam el-Pasha,** once the mosque's luxurious Turkish bath, now furnished as Acre's museum. The **Citadel's** foundations date from Crusader times, although the construction is mostly Turkish. A look at the "crypt", actually the knights' dining hall, will get you right in the spirit of Crusader days.

The northern coast of Israel abounds in beautiful places to sun and swim, but **Nahariyya** is the spot preferred by those who know them all. A cooling stream ripples along a canal in the middle of the town's main street, and shady café tables along the waterfront provide respite from the hot sun. Nahariyya is crowded on Saturdays, so it is better to plan your visit for a weekday. For a trip, take a bus or taxi to ROSH HANIKRA, atop the cliffs on the Lebanese border. A cable car will take you down the cliffside to its base so you can explore the grottoes formed and shaped over thousands of years by the constant washing of the waves.

Tel Aviv – Jaffa

Jaffa (Yafo) has been Jerusalem's port since biblical times, but **Tel Aviv** is completely new. It grew haphazardly to fill the needs of the floods of Jewish immigrants arriving during this century, and soon the throbbing modern metropolis engulfed the sleepy Arab town of Jaffa. Now, with big hotels crowding the sea-front and high-rise blocks spreading through the city, brash and worldly Tel Aviv is the nerve centre of Israel's commercial, industrial and cultural life. It has little of Jerusalem's fascination and beauty, but life here provides a change of pace from the weighty sanctity of the Holy City.

Start your sightseeing from the **observation platform** on the tall office building called the Shalom Tower off Allenby Street; it's the best place for a general view of the urban sprawl. Next, visit the city's modern **Great Synagogue,** not far from the tower. Habimah National Theatre and Mann Auditorium, a short distance from the centre of the city, are the attractive, modern focal points of Israel's cultural life, home of the nation's repertory theatre company and of

TEL AVIV – JAFFA (YAFO)

the famed Israel Philharmonic Orchestra. The Helena Rubinstein Art Pavilion is near Habimah, at 6 Tarsat Boulevard.

As for museums, Tel Aviv has close to two dozen of them, preserving everything from David Ben-Gurion's house to specimens of Bronze Age glass. Several museums are found in the **Ha'Aretz** **Museum** complex in Ramat-Aviv, north of the Yarkon River. Of the others, the Haganah Museum, 23 Rothschild Boulevard, has some interesting exhibits on the military history of the country this century. The Museum of Tel Aviv, 27 Shaul Hamelech Boulevard, has collections of art in various media, and rooms for chamber

Tel Aviv, big town with a global focus: sprawling, bustling, modern.

music concerts. Finally, the **Museum of the Jewish Diaspora** (Beth Hatefutsoth) is a fascinating place. With dioramas and models, photographs and films, the history of the Jewish people from the destruction of the Temple in A.D. 70 to the year 1948 is recounted.

Tel Aviv also boasts a **Dolphinarium** (Charles Clore Park, Herbert Samuel Boulevard). Dolphins and sea lions perform, and the aquarium displays denizens

Helfried Weyer, Nauborn-Wetzlar

of the Red Sea, Mediterranean, and Israel's lakes and rivers.

Tel Aviv explodes with activity on Saturday nights, especially along **Dizengoff Street** between Gordon Street and Dizengoff Square. Old people rest on benches by the fountains in the square, but the young prefer the outdoor cafés and the crowded streets. No one here could mistake Tel Aviv for Jerusalem!

Jaffa, originally a Philistine city, on a promontory over- **83**

looking the Mediterranean, is much more sedate. Fast becoming Tel Aviv's "artists' colony", Jaffa has some of the city's most attractive art galleries, boutiques, cafés and restaurants, most of them near St. Peter's Catholic Church and Monastery. A walk reveals parks and gardens, an Ottoman clock tower and mosque, an archaeological dig, and the Museum of Antiquities of Tel Aviv-Yafo. The old city, which was deserted after the fighting in 1948, has been completely reconstructed.

The popular tourist multivision show, "The Israel Experience", is at 4 Pasteur Street in Old Jaffa.

In the Caliph's Court at Baghdad: scene in Tel Aviv's Diaspora Museum. Right: Shrine of the Book's gleaming dome protects priceless scrolls.

Beth Hatefutsoth, Tel Aviv

What to Do

Museums

On a hill overlooking the historic Valley of the Cross, the **Israel Museum**, Jerusalem, is by far the country's most interesting and comprehensive museum. The collections occupy a series of white, linked pavillions. The large archaeological wing displays the artifacts of man from the dawn of civilization to the Middle Ages.

The **Shrine of the Book**, in a cavelike room underground, contains the most fascinating and important archaeological discoveries in Israel, the Dead Sea Scrolls.

The **Judaica Wing** holds the largest collection of Jewish ceremonial art. The department of **Jewish Ethnography** covers Jewish communities in the Diaspora, as well as the Arab and

Israel Museum holds 5,000 years of history, a lot for one lesson.

Druze communities in Israel. In the **Art Wing** are European paintings, art from farther afield, and the work of Israeli artists.

For a breath of fresh air, stroll in the Billy Rose Sculpture Garden, dotted with works by Moore, Picasso, Lipschitz and others. (See pp. 120–22 for opening hours of all Jerusalem museums.)

In the halls of the medieval citadel, **Tower of David – the Museum of the History of Jerusalem** traces the city's 3,000-year history. The archeological remains date from the Second Temple.

Jerusalem's Islamic Museum, next to El-Aksa Mosque, holds the city's widest-ranging collection of works by Moslem

The Dead Sea Scrolls

In 1947, two Arab shepherd boys searching for a wayward goat stumbled across a hidden cave in the rocks near Qumran on the shores of the Dead Sea. In the cave were eight large clay jars containing several parchment scrolls and fragments wrapped in ancient linen.

Several weeks later, the boys' uncle sold their find for a few pounds to a merchant in Bethlehem. Later, when the scrolls came into the hands of Hebrew University archaeologists in Jerusalem, researchers slowly began to realize that the discovery was one of the most significant ever to have been made in religious history.

Among other scrolls was a complete script of the Old Testament book of Isaiah, 1,000 years older than any previously know codex. Comparing it with modern translations, experts found that the old and new versions were almost exactly the same – a triumph for many scholars as the discovery lent credence to the authority of the biblical writings and demonstrated that years of painstaking effort to faithfully reproduce the ancient texts had been successful.

The Dead Sea Scrolls have still to yield all their secrets. Far from caves and clay jars, most of the priceless documents are now housed in the "Shrine of the Book" in the Israel Museum.

artists, including tiles, carved wood and stone, illuminated manuscripts and some fine calligraphy.

For another collection of Islamic works of art, visit the L.A. Mayer Memorial Institute, 2 Hapalmach Street, where antique firearms and swords add drama to domestic items such as glassware, pottery and jewellery.

Archaeological collections abound in Jerusalem. The **Rockefeller Museum** collection runs from early prehistoric times to 1700 A.D. You can see the bones of Mount Carmel Man, who lived over 100,000 years ago. Smaller archaeological collections are in the Pontifical Bible Institute, Rehov Paul Emil Botta, and around the corner in the Skirball Museum of the Hebrew Union College, 13 King David Street.

The **Old Yishuv Court Museum,** 6 Rehov Or Hayyim, in the Old City's Jewish Quarter, gives a glimpse into the daily life of the "Old Yishuv", the Jewish community living here before the 20th-century. This private-home-turned-museum has a good collection of artisans' implements.

Sports

Most sports are available in Israel, but water activities of all kinds tend to be the most popular. Diving, water-skiing and sailing facilities can be found at most of Israel's seaside resorts.

Warmest for winter swimming is **Eilat** on the Red Sea. This paradise for divers offers equipment for hire, courses for beginners and glass-bottomed boats for enthusiasts who like to admire the fish and keep dry. Of the Mediterranean beaches in the south, **Ashkelon** has a very fine strand. **Bat Yam** and **Herzliyya** are just on the outskirts of Tel Aviv, with the resorts of **Netanya** and **Caesarea** (see p. 79) a little farther north. In the Haifa area, **Nahariyya** (see p. 80) is good.

Israel's largest water theme park is near Tel Aviv, along the Yarkon River. The Galilee also boasts a popular water theme park called Luna Gal, near Ein

Sea of Galilee: Jesus calmed its stormy waters. Today it's a focus for recreation.

Gev. Also worth a visit is the Kibbutz Kalia water park on the Dead Sea where you can swim in the pools or in the Dead Sea, tel.: (02) 936253.

In Jerusalem, the YMCA indoor pool is open all year round. There are also pools at Kiryat HaYovel south of the Mount Herzl area, farther out at Ramat Rachel kibbutz above the Bethlehem road and Kfar Hanofesh in the woods near Yad Vashem, and in all five-star hotels. The swimming season extends from May to September.

Football (soccer) and basketball are well-attended spectator sports, but it's not usually hard to get tickets. There are stadiums at the Hebrew University of Jerusalem and in Tel Aviv.

Many centres offer tennis and, a few, riding facilities; there's an 18-hole golf course at Caesarea.

Shopping

Jerusalem has large and modern department stores as well as eastern bazaars. For the former, try the central triangle of Jerusalem, formed by King George, Jaffa and Ben Yehuda Streets. For handiwork and craft items, Old Jerusalem offers olivewood figurines, gold and silver jewellery, ceramic pieces, trays, cups, Turkish coffee sets and candelabra of copper and brass. Leather articles, hand-woven cloths, embroidered dresses and shirts are beautiful. Many shops carry similar pieces so it's a good idea to shop around – and don't hesitate to bargain!

If you buy inlaid work, be sure the box or backgammon set really has inlay, for decal (transfer) films look very like the real thing – you have got to inspect the piece very closely to detect the difference. In most shops in Old Jerusalem you can have your **89**

Ronald Sheridan, Harrow-on-the-Hill

name – in Latin, Hebrew or Arabic letters – cut from a sheet of gold or silver and made into a pendant or clip.

Among the places specializing in high-quality craft items are Khutzot Hayotzer, just below the Citadel on Jerusalem Brigade Road, and the Jerusalem House of Quality, 12 Hebron Road.

The best leather goods and clothing can be found in Cardo Street, in the Jewish Quarter, and in the Arab shops in the Old City.

Shopping hours are usually from 9 a.m. to 1 p.m. and 4 to 7 p.m., though on the eve of the Sabbath and Jewish holy days shopkeepers may close around 2 p.m. Some shops have a half-day closing on Tuesday afternoons. Jewish shops are closed on Saturday, Moslem ones on Friday, Christian ones on Sunday. The bazaar is active more or less seven days a week, and bargaining is customary.

Tourists can make purchases at advantageous prices in the duty-free shops of Jerusalem (to be found in certain hotels).

Glittering shop windows delight the eye, but on hot days an ice cool drink is as good as gold.

Tax Refunds for Tourists

Tourists can be refunded the Value Added Tax paid on purchases over the equivalent of US$50 in shops registered with the Ministry of Tourism. (These shops display the emblem of two figures carrying a bunch of grapes.) Ask for the requisite form and invoice, and present it with the goods to the official of the Bank Leumi in the departure lounge at Ben Gurien Airport or

Haifa port. They will refund the amount of VAT in US dollars after deducting commission. At other departure points, a customs official will send a VAT refund to your home address.

Nightlife

Though Jerusalem has a few nightclubs and smoke-filled cabarets, its evening entertainments are mostly of a more sedate kind. The open-air **sound and light show** in the Citadel (see p. 122 for times of performance) is well worth while seeing, but dress warmly – everyone underestimates the chill. Tickets are on sale at the Citadel entrance by Jaffa Gate.

On most evenings, **folkdance performances** are given in the Khan theatre, south of the Montefiore Windmill across the street from the railway station. The Khan, a refurbished Ottoman caravanserai, also has a restaurant and bar, and is worthy of a look in itself. There is a YMCA folkdance at 9 p.m. every night except Fridays and Sundays. Get details of current folkdance offerings from one of the Israel Government Tourist Offices.

The larger hotels in West Jerusalem often schedule **folk song evenings** with Israeli performers and perhaps even a jolly audience sing-along. Consult the daily newspapers or the Tourism Ministry's bulletin, *Events in the Jerusalem Region*, for information on shows.

Jerusalem has a rich cultural life at night. A half-dozen halls and theatres host concerts and recitals, drama and ballet. The city's cinemas are located mainly in West Jerusalem. Films are screened in the original language with Hebrew, English or French

92

Immigrants from many countries have added their costumes, dances and songs to Jerusalem's own. Vibrant performances bring them to life.

subtitles. Cinemas are well-attended (often with somewhat brash and noisy crowds), especially on Saturday evenings, and it's a good idea to buy your tickets a half-hour or so in advance.

For **nightclubs,** West Jerusalem's big hotels are the ones with the best shows, which tend to be folkloric rather than titillating. In East Jerusalem, Arabic nightclubs and some restaurants offer intriguing but fairly subdued oriental dancing, plus delightful Arabic music.

Young people out for dancing to rock bands need only stroll around Zion Square and Ben Yehuda Street around 10 o'clock in the evening, letting their ears lead them to the currently popular club. For that cosy café table for two, walk along Rivlin Street, south of Jaffa Road near Bar Kokhba Square, and see which of the little cafés will suit your taste. **93**

Eating Out

Jerusalem's cuisine is as polyglot as its people, and no one would think it strange to find goulash, gefilte fish, *faláfel* and hamburgers on the same menu. Settlers from all over the world brought their native cooking with them, adapted it to the produce of the Holy Land, made it kosher, added a dash of Arabic flavour, and ended up with the astonishing and sometimes bewildering mixture of Jerusalem food.

Breakfast

Those used to a slice of toast and a cup of coffee in the morning may be overwhelmed by a Jerusalem breakfast. Both Arab and Israeli-run hotels tend to present mammoth meals, often weighing down a huge buffet table: eggs cooked several ways, fresh fruits and juices, pickled fish and vegetables, different kinds of olives and cheeses, humus (a chickpea puree), purees of vegetables and beans. sliced tomatoes, a half-dozen kinds of bread, cakes and rolls, yogurt, and even corn flakes. There is a real danger of overeating and ending up back in bed. If you enjoy coffee at breakfast, you can

Purveyors for a dozen cuisines, bazaar shops can please anyone.

always ask for instant if the "freshbrewed" version normally on offer does not appeal. Or you could simply switch to tea.

Lunch

The plenitude of breakfast is matched only by the sturdy Jerusalem lunch, usually the main meal of the day, with a meat course. As certain traditional rules relating to food *(káshrut)* require at least six hours to pass between the eating of meat and the eating of dairy products, Israelis tend to avoid things such as steak with potatoes topped by butter, or cheeseburgers.

If a heavy lunch is too much for you in the summer heat, many cafés and small restaurants have light luncheon plates, salads or

Keeping Kosher

Judaism's dietary laws are observed more often than not in Israel, and so Jews who keep strictly to kosher meals find no problem. Virtually all of the hotels in West Jerusalem serve only kosher meals in their restaurants as a matter of course, and most other dining-places in this part of the city are kosher as well – even the Chinese, Russian and American places.

You will find it nearly impossible to have milk and meat products together at the same meal, but otherwise dinner in a kosher restaurant is likely to be much the same as you're used to at home.

In East Jerusalem the hotels and restaurants generally are not kosher, though the prohibition of pork familiar to Jews is also a Moslem tenet. Seafood must have fins and scales to he kosher, and so you'll find no shellfish in Jewish restaurants. Moslem chefs tend to go along with this prohibition, though the Koran does not specifically ban shellfish from the diet.

cheese dishes. Smoked turkey, which substitutes quite deliciously for the forbidden ham, is a good choice. Pickled vegetables are served at all times and under all circumstances.

Dinner

For Jerusalemites, dinner at home is often a light repast, though the city's restaurants are geared to foreign habits and provide full-course dinners. French, Chinese, German, Italian, Hungarian, Russian and American meals are all easy to come by, and East Jerusalem is full of Arab restaurants. A favourite oriental meat dish is *shwárma,* rounds of lamb stacked on a vertical spit and grilled against a vertical charcoal or gas grill, the cooked outer layer of the meat being sliced off and served when done.

Lamb comes in all forms, including such dubious delicacies as fried brains and stuffed heart. Green salad or a "Turkish salad" of chopped vegetables in a very spicy dressing may accompany your meat dish.

Exotic? After a few bites you may learn how to make it at home.

Desserts are European or Middle Eastern. Many immigrants came from Central Europe, and Viennese-style coffeehouses abound, complete with *Sachertorte* and *Kleine Braune*. Flan is frequently found on dessert menus. But you must

taste the *báklava,* a sweet flaky pastry of ground nuts and honey. *Burma,* a Turkish dessert, is made of shredded wheat rolls stuffed with whole pistachio nuts and soaked in syrup or honey. *Sahlab,* an Arab treat, is a bland milk-and-rose-water pudding.

Snacks

If there is a dish to unite Arabs and Israelis, it is *faláfel,* spiced balls of chick-pea meal deep-fried, mixed with chopped vegetables and peppers, stuffed in half a round of flat *píta* (Eastern) bread, and topped with a few spoonfuls of *takhína,* a sesame seed butter. From morning till night Jerusalemites stop at stands all over the city and pay the small price for this tasty snack.

Fresh-squeezed fruit and vegetable juices are an important thirst-quencher in the hot months, and juice bars can be found with little trouble anywhere in the city.

Beverages

Soft drinks, including some familiar international brands, and a local fizzy mineral water, are on

Attacking a faláfel sandwich demands some mighty manœuvrings.

sale everywhere, competing with fresh juices as thirst-quenchers among devout Moslems, who drink no alcohol.

Coffee and tea are served everywhere, but you must be careful when ordering. Arab cafés will serve you very sweet Turkish coffee unless you ask for it *sókar 'aleel* (with just a pinch of sugar). Your coffee may be perfumed with *hehl* (cardamom seed), a delightful addition. You can often get a glass of "Nes" (instant coffee) instead, if you prefer. Cafés with espresso machines may serve you a fairly tasty cup of "capuccino", which in Jerusalem means coffee with whipped cream. Some cafeterias, snack bars and restaurants serve a local speciality coffee made by pouring hot water into a glass with coffee grounds, called *botz* ("mud"). *Botz* looks, smells, tastes and goes down like its namesake, and should be avoided at all costs. Remember to specify which kind of coffee you want when you order or you may find yourself with a serving of *botz.*

The bottled beer is mostly American-style lager – try *Maccabee* or *Gold Star* – though some hotels and bars have a local dark beer as well. Imported beers **99**

A rolling coffee-shop can follow the crowd: have it Turkish-style or just instant, in a glass.

are available, but are much more expensive than the local brew.

Israeli wines are quite palatable, many being exported and enjoyed abroad. Red, white and rosé – dry or semi-dry and sparkling wines – are available. Two names to remember are Yarden Sauvignon Blanc and Golan Cabernet Sauvignon Red.

Though alcohol is forbidden to Moslems, Christian Arabs often drink *árak*, aniseed-flavoured brandy. With water and ice the *árak* turns a milky colour and is mild enough to drink with the meal, or it can be drunk full-strength as a liqueur. *Golden Arak* is one of the preferred brands. Many Israelis end their meals with *Sabra*, Israel's orange-and-chocolate liqueur, but there are quite a few other brandies and liqueurs to choose from.

When you dine in East Jerusalem, remember that some Arab restaurants do not serve alcoholic drinks at all, but most of the large restaurants do.

To Help You Order…

Could we have a table? **Efshár lekabél shulkhán?**
I'd like a/an/some… **ten li, bevakashá**

beer	**bíra**	olive oil	**shémen záyit**
bread	**lékhem**	pepper	**pilpél**
butter	**khemá**	potatoes	**tapukhéy-adamá**
cheese	**gviná**	rice	**órez**
chips (french fries)	**chips**	rolls	**lakhmaniyót**
		salad	**salát**
coffee	**kafé**	salt	**mélakh**
fish	**dag**	sandwich	**sándwich**
fruit	**peyrót**	soup	**marák**
ice-cream	**glidá**	sugar	**sukár**
lemon	**lemón**	vegetables	**yerakót**
lettuce	**khása**	vinegar	**khómetz**
milk	**khaláv**	water	**máyim**
mustard	**khardál**	wine	**yáyin**

and Read the Menu…

báklava	sweet flaky pastry with nuts	**kréplakh**	dough envelopes with savoury filling
dag malúakh	herring	**lében**	yogurt
éshel	sour milk	**sahlab**	milk and rose-water pudding
faláfel	spiced fried chick-pea paste	**piláf**	Turkish-style rice
gefilte fisch	chopped stuffed carp	**pilpél memulá**	stuffed peppers
khálva	honey, almond and sesame cake	**píta**	flat bread
		shnítzel	veal or turkey, breaded and fried
khamuzím	pickled vegetables		
khúmus	chick-pea puree	**shaménet**	sour cream
kavéd of	chicken liver	**shashlík**	skewered meat and vegetables
kebáb	roast lamb or mutton, or ground meat grilled on wood fire	**shwárma**	vertical-roast lamb
		tarnegól hódu	turkey
kishuim	marrow (zucchini) squash	**takhína**	sesame seed paste sauce

And While You're There...

There's more to Israel than holy sites and historic monuments. Ask anyone who has visited swinging **Eilat**, principal resort of the Sinai region. You can count on year-round sunshine here, and winters are pleasantly warm. The town of about 25,000 lies at the north-eastern tip of the Gulf of Aqaba, an extension of the Red Sea, some 300 kilometres south of Jerusalem. The gulf is rich in spectacular coral formations and fish life, which makes for some of the best snorkelling and scuba diving in the world.

In stark contrast to the colourful dreamlike underwater world of the Red Sea is the barren grandeur of the Sinai Desert. A geological garden of primary rock in many shapes and colours, interlaced by red and white Nubian sandstone and sand dunes. Scattered over this huge area are small Bedouin communities, half nomad, where a few features of the 20th century are woven into a timeless way of life. Many Bedouins have taken to village life, spending summers in their orchards up the valleys. Others have opened businesses, guide tourists or offer their private cars as a cheap Sinai taxi service.

Although Sinai reverted to the Egyptians in 1982, crossing into Eastern Sinai entails only a few formalities. Just south of the border is the **Coral Island** with a 12th-century Crusader castle, newly renovated. A little further on is a lovely narrow inlet known as the **Fjord**, and the **Sun Pool**, an inferno bubbling with hot water.

Follow the road south along the beautiful shores of the Red Sea and stop to rest, and bathe and dive into the waters of the coral reef. Then turn east into the high mountains and visit the 6th-century Greek Orthodox **Monastery of St. Catherine**, a picturesque ensemble of church, dining hall, library, a rare collection of Byzantine icons and a skeleton room. An unforgettable experience is climbing to the top of Mount Sinai before dawn to see the sun rise over the wild peaks in a sea of mist. The more adventurous can hire a Bedouin guide – and a camel for the luggage – and explore the high mountain trails.

Once you've covered the outlying tourist sights, you can concentrate on resort life in Eilat proper – a lively town with a preponderately young citizenry. Try your hand at the wide range of water sports on offer – everything from wind-surfing (board sailing) and deep-sea fishing to jet skiing. Rest up on the beach. Or plunge into that exotic underwater world, so vibrant with colour and light, so full of unsuspected beauties and treasures.

BLUEPRINT for a Perfect Trip

How to Get There

Because of the complexity and variability of the many fares, you should ask the advice of an informed travel agent well before your departure.

BY AIR

Scheduled flights

Daily scheduled flights connect London Heathrow to Ben-Gurion airport at Lod, outside Tel Aviv. The journey takes some 5½ hours.

Daily non-stop service is available from gateway cities in North America (Boston, Chicago, New York). There are also direct flights several times a week from Montreal and Washington, D.C. Many other U.S. and Canadian cities have easy connections through these main points.

Charter Flights and Package Tours

From the United Kingdom. These operate throughout the year. Bookings for Christmas and Easter week need to be made well in advance. Prices vary according to the season, with October to April considered as the "high" season.

It's possible to find a very cheap flight and choose your own accommodation as part of the package deal for a seven-night stay. You can fly from Cardiff, Gatwick, Luton, Birmingham, East Midlands and Manchester. Package holiday flights also go to Eilat on the Red Sea. Your agent will advise you about cancellation insurance.

From North America. The most popular Group-Inclusive Tours (GIT) to Israel last from 9 to 14 days, with three- or four-night extensions to Amsterdam, Athens, London or Rome. They include transport, accommodation, breakfast, transfers, sightseeing and all taxes.

Advanced Booking Charters (ABC) – for visitors to Israel who wish to spend up to four months touring on their own – offer the flight only, between North American cities and Tel Aviv.

Another excellent travel possibility during low season is the One-Stop Inclusive Tour Charter (OTC) with flight and accommodation.

BY SEA

Adriatica lines operate all year round, but the others only sail from June to September. Besides the car ferries from Venice, Naples, Athens or Malta, there are also Mediterranean cruise ships which include Haifa as a port of call on their itinerary. You can also get to Israel in a couple of weeks cruising from Southampton.

When to Go

Spring and autumn are ideal times for a visit to Jerusalem. There should be virtually no rain then with comfortably moderate temperatures. Remember that Jerusalem is up in the Judean hills and is usually cooler than other parts of the country. In winter it gets chilly in Jerusalem and rains frequently. On rare occasions it may even snow. Summer heat is intense, though dry. Sunstroke and dehydration are real dangers everywhere in Israel during the summer.

The following chart gives average monthly temperatures in Jerusalem.

	J	F	M	A	M	J	J	A	S	O	N	D
°C	8	10	12	16	20	22	24	25	23	21	16	11
°F	46	50	54	61	68	72	75	75	73	70	61	52

An A–Z Summary of Practical Information and Facts

A   **AIRPORTS.** Ben Gurion (Lod) airport, about 20 kilometres (12 miles) from Tel Aviv, 45 kilometres (28 miles) from Jerusalem, serves the whole country, although some charter flights from Europe go directly to Eilat. The airport offers many services, including a nursery, post office, restaurants, currency-exchange offices and duty-free shops. An information service, (03) 9712484-8, is open 24 hours a day for flight and tourism inquiries.

Transport: Taxis, buses and *sheruts* (mostly eight-seat Mercedes operating as shared taxis) wait just outside the terminal.

The best way of getting to Jerusalem is by *sherut*, a 40- to 50-minute trip. *Sheruts* leave as soon as they're full, and operate continuously, day and night. Taxis, a bit faster, are notably more expensive. Taxis and *sheruts* will take you to your hotel in Jerusalem at no extra cost; though some drivers may dispute this, it is the law. The bus to Jerusalem leaves about every 30–40 minutes from 6.35 a.m. to 9.40 p.m., though there is no service on Sabbaths (Friday from an hour before sunset until Saturday at sunset) and on holidays. The trip by bus takes an hour, and costs one third of the price of a *sherut*.

Buses of the 222 United Tours company run from the major hotels in Tel Aviv, along Hayarkon Street and via Arlozoroff Railway Station to Ben Gurion Airport. The service operates every 45 minutes from about 4 a.m. to midnight except Sabbaths.

Departure: Tourists are reminded to reconfirm their reservations 72 hours in advance of scheduled departure. When returning to Ben Gurion airport, ask your hotel to reserve a seat in a *sherut* for you, leaving *at least three hours* before your flight time (check-in is a minimum of two hours before departure time); if you check your luggage in at the airline city office (El Al and several other companies) the evening before departure (except Fridays and holidays), you need only reach the airport 1½ hours in advance. For details call El Al, tel. 246725, 1–11 p.m. Sunday to Thursday. The *sherut* will pick you up at your hotel – even in the middle of the night – and get you to the airport in time for the thorough, but courteous, security checks. If you want a bus, they leave from Jerusalem's Central Bus Station every 30–40 minutes between 6 a.m. and 8.30 p.m., Sabbaths excepted. For details, ring the Egged company, tel. 177 022 5555.

A departure tax is levied on every passenger at the check-in desk. Do not have film in your camera at the airport (see PHOTOGRAPHY).

Domestic flights: Jerusalem has its own tiny airport, Atarot (tel. (02) 8333677), although *sherut* service from Ben Gurion airport is so handy that hardly anyone uses it. Arkia (Israel Inland Airlines, Ltd.) operates flights between principal points within Israel using both Ben Gurion airport and the smaller Sde Dov airport at Tel Aviv.

Addresses: El Al: 12 Hillel Street, Jerusalem; tel. (02) 256033.
Arkia: Klal Centre, 97 Jaffa (Yafo) Road, Jerusalem; tel. (02) 255888/234855.

CAMPING. Camping is highly developed in Israel, and you can reach sites by car, caravan (trailer), or even by bus. In Jerusalem, there are shops where you can hire all the necessary camping equipment, from clothing to tables and seats. Tents and cabins are also for hire on the sites themselves, and other facilities such as restaurants or shops, open-air fireplaces, picnic tables, electricity and toilets are always available.

Contact the Israeli Camping Union: P.O. Box 53, Nahariyya (north of Haifa); tel. (04) 925392, fax: (04) 928646.

CAR HIRE. See also DRIVING. You must be 21 years of age and have held a driving licence for at least one year. Rates include public liability insurance, property damage, fire and theft, but not the deductable portion of collision coverage, for which you may choose to pay a small extra charge. Personal injury coverage for the driver is not included. If you pay by credit card, you do not have to give a deposit equal to the estimated rental charge. If you pay by card or in foreign currency, you are exempt from the VAT added to the total invoice. Drive a hired car only on asphalted roads – insurance coverage does not apply if you drive on back roads or tracks.

CHILDREN. Children are the future of Israel, and in a country of only just over 5 million people which favours population increase, they are a blessing. Yours will be accepted happily, and your hotel staff will be glad to arrange for a baby-sitter at night.

Particularly recommended for children in Jerusalem is the **Tisch Family Zoological Gardens**, on the route of bus No. 26. It is located at: The Zoo Drive, Manhat, P.O. Box 898, 91008 Jerusalem, tel. (02) 430111, fax: (02) 430122.

C   The **Museum of Natural History** at 6 Mohliver Street in the German colony district has lots of working models, as well as displays of animals and birds from all over Israel (bus No. 4, 14 or 18). tel. (02) 631116.

For young children, the **Islamic Art Museum** (L.A. Mayer Memorial Institute for Islamic Art) at 2 HaPalmakh Street offers interesting exhibits, including a collection of automats (bus No. 15). tel. (02) 661291.

The **Jerusalem Theatre**, the **Israel Museum** and the **International Cultural Centre for Youth** have programmes, films and spectacles for children and young people. The Youth Centre puts on folklore and folk-dancing shows every Saturday evening.

Finally seek out the **playground** in the distant Kiryat HaYovel quarter (on the way to Hadassah Hospital), for the world's most fearsome children's slide. The gigantic black-and-white spike-headed monster has three scarlet tongues down which children glide (bus No. 18, 20, 23 and 27).

CIGARETTES, CIGARS, TOBACCO. Jerusalem's tobacco shops sell most internationally known brands of cigarettes, plus a selection of imported cigars and a dozen different kinds of pipe tobacco (mostly Dutch). Imported cigarettes cost twice as much as local brands. The Sabbath is a "non-smoking day" in many restaurants.

CLOTHING. Dress is informal in Israel, as the heat makes jacket-and-tie formality impossible. But religious decorum demands that women have shoulders and heads covered in mosques and synagogues. Short skirts and shorts or sleeveless blouses and dresses on women are not acceptable in holy places.

In summer's intense heat, breezy cotton clothing is best, with a light pullover for the evening cool. A broad-brimmed hat and sunglasses are absolutely essential. In winter, Jerusalem can be wet and chilly; bring a light raincoat in January and make sure to have a comfortable pair of shoes (sandals in summer).

COMMUNICATIONS

Post offices in Israel handle letters and parcels, and also telephone, fax, telegraph and telex operations. Most Jerusalem letter boxes are red English-style pillar boxes. Others are white and blue and bear the postal symbol of a leaping deer. Shops and kiosks which sell stamps, and newspaper shops which have a post office agency, carry the same sign.

Hours (Central Post Office): Sunday to Thursday: 8 a.m. to 6 p.m. Friday: 8 a.m. to 2 p.m. Closed on Saturdays and public holidays.

Branch post offices are normally open 8 a.m.–12.30 p.m. daily and 3.30–6 p.m. except Wednesdays. On Fridays most open until 1 or 2 p.m.

Poste restante (general delivery): If you don't know exactly where you'll be staying, you can have your mail sent poste restante to whichever town is most convenient. In Jerusalem, use the Central Post Office (see below).

It can take around 1½ weeks for a letter to reach you from Europe or North America. Have your passport with you for identification.

Telegrams, Telex and Fax: Telegrams can be sent 24 hours a day from Jerusalem's Central Post Office, or by phoning 171. Telex and fax offices, in the same building, are open during normal post once hours. If the party you're contacting has a telex or fax machine, send your message this, way – it's much cheaper than by telegraph. You can find their number in directories at the office. tel. (02) 290774.

Telephone: You can dial a call to any part of the country from a public telephone, using the necessary city prefix. You'll need telephone tokens, *asimonim*, for the old type of public phones and telecards for the newer models. They're on sale at some newspaper kiosks and in post of fixes but they're difficult to find easily if you need one and are in a hurry. Do not insert more than three tokens at a time, as they tend to get stuck, but watch out that there is at least one spare all the time. Using a public telephone is generally cheaper than calling from a hotel or a shop. International calls can be made from post offices and international telephone centres, and direct from the blue-and-yellow public pay phones using pre-paid telecards only. Hotels often add a big surcharge to the cost of an international call.

Jerusalem's Central Post Office: 23 Jaffa Road; tel. (02) 290647.
East Jerusalem: Saladin Street, opposite Herod's Gate; tel. (02) 290686.

COMPLAINTS. Jerusalem's hotels, restaurants and shops are so used to welcoming foreign visitors that complaints are usually handled satisfactorily on the spot. If you have to appeal to a higher authority, the Israel Government Tourist Office and the Municipal Tourist Information Office (see TOURIST INFORMATION OFFICES) have a special form to register complaints.

CONSULATES and EMBASSIES. Jerusalem is Israel's capital city, though most foreign nations still maintain their embassies in Tel Aviv. Because Jerusalem was once divided, some nations have consulates in both **109**

C parts of the city. Closed Saturday and Sunday. Office hours are generally from 9 a.m. to 12 noon, but some will answer between 4 and 6 p.m.

Australia, Embassy: Beil-Europa, 37, Shaul Hamelech Blvd, Tel Aviv; tel. (03) 6950451.

Canada, Embassy: 220 Hayarkon Street, Tel Aviv; tel. (03) 5272929, fax: (03) 5272333.

Great Britain, (and citizens of Eire) Consulate-General: Tower House, Kikar Remez Street (near Railway Station), Jerusalem; tel. (02) 717724/719036.

Consulate-General (main office): 19 Nashashibi Street, Sheikh Jarrah, Jerusalem; tel. (02) 828281/828482/828483, fax: 322368.

Embassy: 192 Hayarkon Street, Tel Aviv; tel. (03) 5249171, fax: 5243313.

Consular Section: 6th Floor, Migdalor Building, 1 Ben Yehuda Street, Tel Aviv; tel. (03) 5100166/5100497, fax: (03) 5101167.

South Africa, Embassy: 2 Kaplan Street, Tel Aviv; tel. (03) 5252566.

U.S.A., Consulate-General: 18 Agron Street, Jerusalem (Consular Section: Nablus Road); tel. (02) 253288.

Consulate-General: Nablus Road, Jerusalem; tel. (02) 253288.

Embassy: 71 Hayarkon Street, Tel Aviv; tel. (03) 5174338, fax: (03) 5102444.

CONVERTER CHARTS. For fluid and distance measures, see page 112. Israel uses the metric system.

Length

Weight

Temperature

CRIME. In general, Jerusalem must be one of the safest cities in the world, though pickpockets are a real menace in crowded buses and in the narrow streets of the bazaar. Wallets, handbags, even rings and wrist-watches can disappear in the throng.

By all means stay away from illegal money changers, who sometimes cheat or rob visitors while making black market transactions.

In beach resorts, thieves have been known to roam the sands on the look-out for passports, money and hotel-room keys, so secure these items.

DRIVING IN ISRAEL
To take your car into Israel you will need:
● a valid driving licence (see below)
● car registration papers
● an insurance certificate

You must have either an International Driving Licence or a national driving licence issued by a country which recognizes the Israeli licence. (If your national licence is in a language other than English or French, you must get a Hebrew translation or confirmation of it.)

Driving conditions: There is a high rate of accidents and drivers take big risks, so watch out for everything: overloaded trucks, drivers who turn right but put out a left blinker, vehicles without lights, etc. Driving is especially dangerous after the first rains, as all the dirt and grease accumulated during the dry season form a slippery layer on streets; at the same time, drains get blocked and the roads become rivers.

Roads: Except for the excellent motorway (expressway) between Tel Aviv and Jerusalem and the coastal highway from Ashdod to Acre, Israel's roads are normal two-lane ones. They're well maintained, but not built for high-speed driving.

Parking: To park in Jerusalem's streets, you'll need a parking card (sold at the entrance of large parking lots and by lottery-ticket or newspaper vendors). Tear off the three tabs on the card which indicate the month, date and hour you park, and display the card in the window.

Note that police place wheel clamps on illegally parked cars.

Traffic Police, see POLICE.

Fuel and Oil. Service stations are not difficult to find in the modern sections of East and West Jerusalem, and towns along the country's highways usually have at least one station. If stations in West Jerusalem are closed 111

D because of a Sabbath or holiday, drive to the East, where stations are liable to be open (or vice versa). Types of fuel available are 96-octane, 91-octane, diesel and unleaded.

Fluid measures

Distance

Automobile Club: For help in getting an International Driving Licence or other motoring matters, contact the Automobile Club and Touring Association of Israel (M.E.M.S.I.):

Jerusalem: Klal Centre, Room 226, 97 Jaffa Street; tel. (02) 247080/250661. Tel Aviv (head office): 20 Harakevet Street; tel. (03) 5641111, fax: (03) 5609131.

Breakdowns: A breakdown in the merciless heat of summer can be unpleasant, but although Israel's roads are not heavily travelled, it probably won't take long to get a ride with a passing motorist, or police patrol. If you're driving a hired car, contact the rental agency before having repairs made, except for minor ones such as a flat tyre.

DRUGS. The use of drugs is considered a serious problem in Israel, especially among young people. Smoking hashish means immediate eviction from kibbutzes and other places where young visitors may go, and very often, if the case is referred to the police, eviction from Israel. The buying and possession of drugs, if discovered, could entail prison sentences.

E **ELECTRIC CURRENT.** Israel's current is 220-volt, 50-cycle, as in Europe. Sockets generally take two- or three-pronged European plugs.

EMERGENCIES. The police emergency number in Jerusalem, Tel Aviv and Haifa is 100. Depending on the nature of the emergency, see the separate entries in this section such as Medical Care, Consulates, etc.

ENTRY FORMALITIES and CUSTOMS CONTROLS. You will need a valid passport to enter Israel. If you plan to visit an Arab country later, be sure the immigration official puts the visa stamp on an immigration form rather than in your passport; most Middle-Eastern countries do not accept passports bearing Israeli stamps. Your entry stamp is good for a stay of three months.

Don't lose the visitor's card that you fill out when entering the country; you may have to show it in the event of a security check or when changing money. It must be handed back at customs upon departure.

Ben Gurion airport uses the "Red" and "Green" channel customs procedure, and tourists with the following items may pass right through the "Green" channel (figures for passengers on return home are given afterwards):

Into:	Cigarettes		Cigars		Tobacco	Spirits		Wine
Israel	250	or	250 g.	or	250 g.	1 l.	and	2 l.
Australia	200	or	250 g.	or	250 g.	1 l.	and	1 l.
Canada	200	and	50	and	900 g.	1.1 l.	or	1.1 l.
Eire	200	or	50	or	250 g.	1 l.	and	2 l.
N. Zealand	200	or	50	or	250 g.	1.1 l.	and	4.5. l.
S. Africa	400	and	50	and	250 g.	1 l.	and	2 l.
U.K.	200	or	50	or	250 g	1 l.	and	2 l.
U.S.A.	200	and	100	and	*			
* a reasonable quantity								

When carrying cameras and cine-cameras (one of each plus U.S.$ 125 worth of films and video cassettes), portable radios and similar items, use the "Red" channel even though these goods are supposed to be duty-free. Note that video cameras are subject to a deposit of up to U.S.$1,000, depending on the value of the camera.

When you leave Israel, you will be asked to check your luggage thoroughly to make certain no one has put anything in it without your knowledge. There's also a good chance that an official will spot-check your bags.

Currency restrictions: You can bring any amount of local and foreign currency into Israel (declaration recommended), and take out local and foreign currencies up to the amount imported and declared. Don't change large amounts of money into shekels, as you may only reconvert up to the

E equivalent of U.S.$100 on departure unless you can show bank receipts proving the original conversion.

G **GUIDES and INTERPRETERS.** You can hire a guide or interpreter by contacting a travel agency. Also, the *Golden Pages* telephone directory lists

individual guides under the heading "Guide Service". A one-day tour of the city in a private car can easily be arranged. Official guides wear a circular badge, and one may approach you as you enter a tourist area. Be sure to settle the fee in advance. Some taxi drivers are licensed

guides. If you see the tourist office symbol of two men bearing a huge bunch of grapes suspended from a pole on the taxi door, chances are that the driver is a licensed guide.

H **HAIRDRESSERS'.** There are plenty of barbers' shops, hairdressers' and beauty salons throughout the country, but an advance appointment is usually advisable. Prices vary greatly, and a humble local barber may charge only a fraction of what customers at a large hotel's shop must pay.

HITCH-HIKING. Hitch-hiking is popular in Israel, and safe so long as you follow the normal precautions. Women should not hitch alone. Don't hitch-hike at night if it can be avoided, and don't hitch-hike in areas where there are disturbances. Many soldiers and other Israelis wait near bus stops on the highways, hoping for a lift. If no one stops, they can still climb aboard a bus.

HOTELS, HOSPICES, KIBBUTZES and YOUTH HOSTELS. The accommodation desk at Ben Gurion airport can help you find a hotel room if you've arrived without a reservation.

Israel Government Tourist Offices distribute a free guide to the country's hotels published by the Israel Hotel Association. Hotel bills (including restaurant charges) settled with foreign currency, traveller's cheques, credit card or Eurocheque are exempt from Value Added Tax.

The room price includes breakfast, usually a substantial one. Children stay at reduced rates: 50% reduction up to the age of six, 30% off for those between six and 12. Air-conditioned rooms are no extra.

West Jerusalem has the newest and largest hotels, all with kosher restaurants. East Jerusalem has several large hotels, some charming older **114** ones, and a good selection of moderately priced establishments.

Hospices: Various Christian denominations have for centuries provided inexpensive places for pilgrims to stay. You do not have to subscribe to any particular belief to stay in a hospice. Rooms and facilities vary greatly, from plain dormitories to comfortable rooms with bath. Meals are often available as well. Tourist offices in Israel and abroad have lists of hospices, or you can write to the Israel Pilgrimage Committee or the Christian Information Centre (see below).

Kibbutzes: A number of kibbutzes have comfortable three- and four-star hotels on their grounds, operated by kibbutz members. Details of the inns are published in the hotel directory, *Israel Tourist Hotels.*

Youth hostels: Israel has around 30 hostels, a third of them in or near Jerusalem. Hostels are open to everyone regardless of age, marital status, occupation or religion.

Addresses:

Israel Pilgrimage Committee, 23 Hillel Street, 11th Floor, Jerusalem; tel. (02) 754907.

Christian Information Centre, Jaffa Gate, Old City, Jerusalem; tel. (02) 272692, fax: (02) 286417.

Kibbutz Inns, 90 Ben Yehuda, Tel Aviv; tel. (03) 5246161, fax: (03) 5230527.

Israel Youth Hostel Association, 3 Dorot Rishonim Street, Jerusalem, tel. (02) 252706, fax: (02) 250676.

JAY-WALKING. Always use cross-walks and obey traffic signals. Jay-walking is illegal in Israel, and transgressors are subject to fines.

LANGUAGE. The official languages of Israel are Hebrew (by far the most widely spoken) and Arabic. English is spoken or at least understood by most of the people tourists deal with. Because many Israelis were born and raised in other countries, Jerusalem's streets and parlours echo with a symphony – or cacophony – of languages including German, French, the Slavic languages and Spanish.

Transcription from Hebrew and Arabic characters to Latin ones adds a further dimension of confusion, and you may see as many as four different spellings of one Hebrew or Arabic word. Place names are another problem. Gates in the city walls, streets, holy sites, and even towns may have a different name in each language: Jerusalem, Yerushalayim, El Kuds. But,

L though it sounds at first like the Tower of Babel, you should have little problem getting around in the city.

The Hebrew alphabet is used for biblical Hebrew, modern Hebrew and Yiddish. The attractive flow of Arabic script is easy on the eyes but hard on the mind, as Arabic letters may have four different shapes depending on whether the character comes at the beginning, middle or end of a word or is used by itself. In both Hebrew and Arabic, only the consonants are written in most cases.

LAUNDRY and DRY-CLEANING. In the busy summer months it may take three or four days to have clothing dry-cleaned, at other times only two days. Same-day service is available at an extra charge.

All hotels can arrange for your laundry and dry-cleaning to be done. The large ones have their own laundries. In medium-size and smaller hotels, try striking a bargain directly with the chamber-maid as this sometimes results in very fast and very inexpensive service. Lightweight garments washed and hung up in the heat of an Israeli summer will dry in about an hour.

M **MAPS.** Government Tourist Offices outside Israel are the best source of free maps. The offices in Jerusalem are sometimes undersupplied with the good pictorial, multicoloured map of the city published by the Ministry of Tourism. Car hire firms will provide you with simplified city and country maps when you rent a car, but a better highway map is published by Bank Hapoalim and given away at Government Tourist Offices and branches of the bank.

MEDICAL CARE. If your home insurance cannot be extended to foreign countries, you may want to take out special travel insurance to cover yourself in case of accident, illness or hospitalization during your trip.

By far the most prevalent malady among tourists in Israel is overexposure to sun and heat. You must *not* ignore the sun. Take sunbathing in short half-hour periods at first, and use lotion or sun cream lavishly in summer. No less dangerous is the threat of dehydration, as you lose surprising quantities of body moisture to the dry air without even noticing it. Drink water and other beverages at every opportunity in the hot months, even if you don't feel particularly thirsty. Sunstroke and heat exhaustion are serious 116 ailments – even potentially fatal – though they are easily avoided by tourists who monitor the amount of sun and fluid loss to which they are subjected. Wear sunglasses and a broad-brimmed hat, and tan your feet slowly before wearing sandals all day.

Beware of flies in the Judean desert; one kind causes serious poisoning. It does not occur frequently, but it is well to remember to mention having been in the area if something like a wound that fails to heal appears.

It's best to inquire also, when going to the Red Sea, about poisonous fish and crustaceans – they can be beautiful, but dangerous.

For emergency medical and dental care in Jerusalem, Tel Aviv and Haifa, call the first-aid service of Magen David Adom, the "Red Shield of David", equivalent to the Red Cross. Outside of normal operating hours (see below), they will put you in touch with a doctor or dentist.

The *Jerusalem Post* carries listings of pharmacies and hospital clinics which take turns staying open all night.

Magen David Adom First Aid Centre in Jerusalem is in Romema near the Central Bus Station; open on Fridays and on the eves of holidays from 9 to 12 p.m., and Saturdays and holidays from 10 a.m. to 2 p.m. and 3 to 6 p.m.

Emergency medical and dental telephone number: 101.

MEETING PEOPLE. Though they may squabble among themselves, Jerusalemites have a ready welcome for foreign tourists no matter what their nationality or religion. The greeting you get may be somewhat more sober and dignified than ebullient and smiling, but this is typical of the spirit of the Holy City, and may also have something to do with the complex and preoccupying problems its citizens face daily. *Shalom* (peace) is the word that begins and ends every conversation in West Jerusalem, with *shabbat shalom* taking its place on the Jewish Sabbath. In East Jerusalem, say *salaam aleikum* (peace with you); answer: *aleikum salaam* (with you, peace) or *meh eh salameh* (with peace), or use the simpler *Allah yisahil tarikak* – "God make your road even" (greeting when meeting someone on his way). In an Arab restaurant you can delight new-found friends with the toast *meh-heh-beh!* (with love!), while in a West Jerusalem restaurant the words are *lekhayim!* (to life!) and *bteh-avon (bon appétit)*.

MONEY MATTERS

Currency: The Israeli unit of currency is the *New Israeli Shekel* (abbreviated *NIS*), divided into 100 *agorot*.

Coins: 1 agora, 5 and 10 agorot, ½, 1 and 5 new shekel.

Banknotes: 10, 20, 50, 100 and 200 New Israeli Shekels.

For currency restrictions, see ENTRY FORMALITIES AND CUSTOMS CONTROLS.

Banking hours: Sunday, Tuesday and Thursday: 8.30 a.m. to 12.30 p.m. and 4 to 5.30 p.m. Monday and Wednesday: 8.30 a.m. to 12.30 p.m. Fridays and the eves of holidays: 8.30 a.m. to 12 noon. Closed on Saturdays and Jewish religious and national holidays.

In West Jerusalem hotels, subsidiary bank offices have longer hours. In East Jerusalem, money-changers' offices are open during daylight hours, with some offices closing on Fridays, others on Sundays. The currency-exchange desks at Ben Gurion airport are always open.

Currency Exchange and Tax Exemption: Now that Israel's stratospheric inflation rate has come down, tourists no longer need be so cautious about changing money. However, if you pay hotel and car hire bills in foreign currency (cash, traveller's cheques, credit card), or by Eurocheque, you will not be charged Value Added Tax.

Tax Refunds: Tourists will be refunded the Value Added Tax paid on items above the equivalent of US$50 purchased in shops registered with the Minstry of Tourism. Present the goods, with a form supplied by the shop, to the Bank Leumi official at Ben Gurion Airport or Haifa port, and a VAT refund will be paid in US dollars less commission. At other departure points, the VAT refund will be sent to your home address.

Credit Cards and Traveller's Cheques: Internationally recognized credit cards and traveller's cheques are accepted by car hire agencies, and the better hotels and restaurants. If you pay by traveller's cheque, you may get change in shekels. Take your passport for identification.

N **NEWSPAPERS and MAGAZINES.** Besides daily papers in Hebrew and Arabic you will find the *Jerusalem Post* on news-stands every day except Saturday; Friday's edition of the *Post* has a special magazine supplement with feature articles, a calendar of events and a guide to entertainment. The *International Herald Tribune* tends to reach Jerusalem the day following publication, and is sold in hotels and at street-side newspaper stands. Other papers and magazines distributed internationally are also easy to find.

P **PHOTOGRAPHY.** Shops that specialize in photography (not only the sale of film) will readily give you hints on what to do and what to use in

Jerusalem. Note that the light in this region with its ultra-violet rays tends to bring out the purple too much, so use, if possible, a UV filter. The best time for photography is 8 a.m. to noon, and at sunset.

Photography is a sensitive subject in Jerusalem, and not just because of the clear and brilliant Israeli sun; taking photographs is not allowed at or near some holy sites on the Sabbath. In the ultra-orthodox quarters – the Bukharian Quarter, Ge'ula and Mea She'arim – even *carrying* or *touching* a camera is prohibited on the Sabbath. Orthodox Jews and Moslems make fascinating subjects for photographs, but you must never take pictures without asking first, even if you shoot from a distance. Anything having to do with military security is off limits to photographers, including airports and docks.

POLICE. Israel has a national police force to maintain law and order in all cities, towns and the countryside. Uniforms are khaki in summer and dark blue in winter. Most officers speak some English and are glad to help with any problems.

At traffic intersections, obey the pedestrian signals. Pairs of police-women patrol the streets in West Jerusalem's central district and fine on the spot those who cross streets contrary to the signals.

In emergencies, dial 100 to reach Jerusalem's Police Headquarters, on Heshin Street, off Jaffa (Yafo) Road in the Russian Compound.

PUBLIC HOLIDAYS and SABBATHS. Jerusalem is a calendar-printer's nightmare, for each religious sect uses its own system of years and dates, and it is no exaggeration to say that if you observed them all, you'd celebrate New Year's Day at least a half-dozen times in one year. Most of these holidays cannot be matched up with the normal (Gregorian) calendar because they are figured in lunar months, or are moveable feasts. The best you can do is keep an eye on local newspapers and events listings. During celebrations of several days, shops and offices run by observers of the holiday may be closed on the first and last days of the festivities, and perhaps open for shorter hours the rest of the time.

The Jewish Sabbath *(shabbat)*, starting at sunset Friday and lasting until sunset on Saturday, is more strictly observed than is the day of rest in most other countries. All Jewish shops and businesses close, most public transport ceases, and the country is brought nearly to a standstill. In Orthodox quarters, driving of cars, carrying or using a camera or writing implement, **119**

P pushing a button or flipping a switch, smoking or in any way kindling fire, and anything else which can be looked upon as work, is banned.

Moslems' holy day starts on Thursday at sunset and continues until sunset on Friday; Christians observe the day of rest all day on Sunday.

R **RADIO and TV.** Israel has six radio channels, broadcast on AM (medium wave), FM and short wave frequencies. News in English is given four times a day – at 7 a.m., 1 p.m., 5 p.m. and 8 p.m. – on 576 and 1458 khz. Jordan Radio, from nearby Amman, also features some programmes and news bulletins in English. The Voice of America and BBC World Service can be heard on the AM band when conditions are good.

Both Israeli and Jordanian television stations broadcast in English, Hebrew and Arabic.

The *Jerusalem Post Magazine*, included with the Friday edition of the newspaper, has full radio and television listings for the week to come.

RELIGIOUS SERVICES. Going to a service in Jerusalem has special significance for every visitor. Government Tourist Offices can give you a booklet which lists synagogues and churches with their addresses and times of services. It's worth confirming the latter to avoid any disappointment. The Christian Information Centre at Jaffa Gate has most comprehensive lists of Christian holy places and services, and the Friday edition of the *Jerusalem Post* gives the times of services.

S **SIESTA.** The mid-afternoon snooze is well established in Jerusalem's daily life, and most shops and offices close for at least two hours between 12.30 or 1 p.m. and about 4 p.m. As the midday meal is customarily the largest one of the day, a rest afterwards during the hottest hours is both sensible and healthful.

SIGHTSEEING HOURS
Basilica of the Agony: 8.30 a.m. to 12 noon and 2.30 p.m. to 6 p.m. from April to October, 8.30 a.m. to 12 noon and 2.30 p.m. to 5 p.m. from November to March.
Cathedral and Convent of St. James: 6.30 to 7.15 a.m. on weekdays; 3 to 3.30 p.m. on Saturdays and Sundays.
Church of Mary Magdalene (Russian): 10 a.m. to 11.30 a.m. Tuesdays and Thursdays only.

Church and Seminary of St. Anne: 8 a.m. to 12 noon and 2 to 5 p.m. in winter, 8 a.m. to 12 noon and 2 to 6 p.m. in summer.

City of David: 9 a.m. to 4 p.m. Saturday to Thursday; 9 a.m. to 1 p.m. Friday.; closed Sunday.

Garden Tomb: 8 a.m. to 12 noon and 2.30 to 5 p.m., Monday to Saturday; closed on Sundays except for service at 9 a.m.

Islamic Museum (Temple Mount): 10 a.m. to 5 p.m., closed Fridays and Moslem holidays (note: only Moslems may enter Temple Mount after 4 p.m.)

Israel Museum and Shrine of the Book: 10 a.m. to 5 p.m. Sunday, Monday, Wednesday and Thursday; 4 p.m. to 10 p.m. Tuesday; 10 a.m. to 2 p.m. Friday and Saturday. Free guided tours in English: 10 a.m. Sunday, Monday and Wednesday.

Tower of David – the Museum of the History of Jerusalem (Citadel): 10 a.m. to 5 p.m. Sunday to Thursday; 10 a.m. to 2 p.m. Friday and Saturday. Guided tours in English: 11 a.m. Sunday to Thursday.

Knesset: 8.30 a.m. to 2.30 p.m. on Sundays and Thursdays except during public holiday periods (bring passport).

L.A. Mayer Memorial Institute for Islamic Art: 10 a.m. to 5 p.m. Sunday, Monday, Wednesday and Thursday; 4 to 8 p.m. Tuesday; 10 a.m. to 2 p.m. Friday, Saturday and holidays.

Model of Second-Temple Jerusalem (Holyland Hotel): 8 a.m. to 8 p.m. in summer, 8 a.m. to 4 p.m. in winter, daily.

Mosque of Makhpelah (Hebron): 7.30 to 11.30 a.m. and 1 to 2.30 p.m. and 3 to 5.30 p.m. daily except Friday.

Museum of the Jewish Diaspora (Bet HaTefutsot, Tel Aviv): 10 a.m. to 5 p.m., Sunday to Thursday; 10 a.m. to 7 p.m. Wednesday; 9 a.m. to 2 p.m. Friday; closed Saturday.

Museum of Natural History: 8.30 a.m. to 6 p.m. Monday to Thursday; 8.30 a.m. to 1 p.m. Sunday; closed Friday and Saturday.

Old Yishuv Court Museum: 9 a.m. to 2 p.m., Sunday to Thursday.

Pontifical Biblical Institute: 9 a.m. to 2 p.m. except Sundays and Catholic holidays.

Rockefeller Museum: 10 a.m. to 2 p.m. Friday and Saturday; 10 a.m. to 5 p.m. Sunday to Thursday.

Shrine of the Book (Israel Museum): same as Museum.

Simon Peter's house and **Capernaum's synagogue** (Capernaum): 8.30 a.m. to 4.15 p.m. daily.

S **Sound and Light Show** (Citadel): Monday, Wednesday and Saturday at 9.30 p.m. in English, one hour earlier in winter.

Temple Mount: 8 a.m. to 4 p.m. daily except Friday, when the Mount is closed during Moslem prayer times.

The Tisch Family Zoological Gardens, Jerusalem: 10 a.m. to 5 p.m. Monday and Thursday; 12 noon to 5 p.m. Sunday, Tuesday and Wednesday; 10 a.m. to 2 p. m. Friday; 10 a.m. to 5 p.m. Saturday.

Tombs of the Prophets: 8 a.m. to 3 p.m. daily except Saturday.

Tombs of the Sanhedrin: 9 a.m. to sunset daily except Saturday.

YMCA (lift): 9 a.m. to 2 p.m. weekdays; 9 a.m. to 1 p.m. Friday and Saturday; closed Sunday.

STREET NAMES. There is something resembling confusion in street names of Jerusalem, written in Hebrew, Arabic, and as often as not, English. The Hebrew word for street is *Rehov*. King George Street, for example, can be called just King George Street, or alternatively HaMelekh George Street, Rehov King George or Rehov HaMelekh George. The only rule: the name itself is what matters, i.e. (King) George. So in this book we have kept to the English forms – which is, in fact, what you'll probably be using most.

T **TIME DIFFERENCES.** The chart below shows the time differences between Israel and various cities in winter. In summer, clocks are put one hour ahead (GMT + 3).

New York	London	**Jerusalem**	Johannesburg	Sydney	Auckland
5 a.m.	10 a.m.	**noon**	noon	9 p.m.	11 p.m.

TIPPING. Israel is very egalitarian in spirit, and tipping is not a hollowed institution among its citizens. You needn't tip taxi drivers, or waiters in restaurants who add a service charge to your bill (if not included, a few coins will suffice). Some further suggestions:

Porter, per bag	U.S.$1
Maid, per week	U.S.$5
Tour guide	5%
Hairdresser/Barber	10%

TOILETS. Public toilets are scattered throughout East and West Jerusalem, in the busier sections. Signs at streetcorners nearby point the way in Hebrew, Arabic and English. Toilets may be marked *W.C.* (for "water closet"), *00* or *Toilet,* with male and female silhouettes.

TOURIST INFORMATION OFFICES. Israel Government Tourist Offices (I.G.T.O.) in other countries, and Tourist Information Offices in Israel are ready to help with maps, brochures and all sorts of information.

Canada: 180 Bloor Street West, Suite 700, Toronto, Ontario M5S 2V6; tel. (416) 964 3784, fax: 001 416 961 3962.

South Africa: 5th floor, Nedbank Gardens, 33 Bath Avenue, Rosebank, P.O. Box 52560, Saxonwold 2132, Johannesburg; tel. (011) 788 1700, fax: (011) 447 3104.

United Kingdom: 18 Great Marlborough Street, London W1V 1AF; tel. (071) 434 3651, fax. (071) 437 0527.

U.S.A.: 19th Floor, 350 Fifth Avenue, New York, NY 10118; tel. (212) 560 0639/0600, fax: (212) 629 4368.

6380 Wilshire Boulevard 1700, Los Angeles, CA 90048; tel. (213) 658 7240/7462/7463, fax: (213) 658 6543.

5 South Wabash Avenue, Chicago, IL 60603; tel. (312) 782 4306/7/8, fax: (312) 782 1243.

12700 Park Central Drive, Dallas, TX 75251; tel. (214) 991 9097/8, fax: (214) 392 3521.

25 SE 2nd Avenue, Suite 745, Miami, FL 33131; tel. (305) 539 1919/8222, fax: (305) 539 1311.

1100 Spring St, NW Suite 440, Atlanta, GA 30309; tel. (404) 875 9924/5, fax: (404) 875 9926.

In Jerusalem, Government Tourist Offices are at:
24 King George Street; tel. (02) 754912/754888/754910
Jaffa Gate in the Old City; tel. (02) 282295/6.

The Jerusalem Municipal Tourist Information Office:
17 Jaffa Road; tel. (02) 258844.

TOURS. See also GUIDES AND INTERPRETERS. You can learn all about Jerusalem without spending a single shekel by going on one of the many free tours organized by the Jerusalem Municipality and many other civic **123**

T and religious groups. Tours are especially plentiful during religious festival periods. Check *Events in the Jerusalem Region,* a free bulletin of current events handed out in hotels and tourist information offices.

Tour companies and travel agencies offer city tours at reasonable prices, and these provide an easy and comfortable way to see the sights in outlying areas. Those with time to visit other parts of the country should consider going with a group if their destination is within the West Bank territories. Tour operators keep well up on sensitive areas, and steer clear of trouble.

TRANSPORT

Buses: When Jerusalem was reunified in 1967, it had two bus companies. It still does. East Jerusalem is served from the terminal called the Old City Bus Station, on Sultan Suleiman Street near Damascus Gate. Bus No. 22 goes to Jaffa Gate, Talpiot, Rachel's Tomb and Bethlehem; No. 23 will take you to Hebron; and No. 75 climbs to the top of the Mount of Olives. The No. 99 tourist bus shuttles between all the major tourist sights, taking you to 35 focal points of the city – in the centre and on the outskirts – from a stop near Jaffa Gate. The Circular Line runs every 2 hours from 10 a.m. to 4 p.m. Sunday to Thursday and from 10 a.m. to 12 noon on Fridays and the day before any public holiday. For information ring (02) 253454, 254198, 304868 or 304422.

West Jerusalem's Central Bus Station, on Jaffa Road in the Etz Haim quarter, handles traffic to the greater part of Jerusalem and to other Israeli cities and towns. Bus service is suspended in West Jerusalem and throughout Israel on the Jewish Sabbath and on Jewish holidays. Arab-operated buses in East Jerusalem run every day.

Bus services in the main cities start at about 5 a.m. and finish around 11.30 p.m.

Taxis: Most taxis belong to agencies and are well controlled. Some drivers cannot resist trying their luck on tourists, however, and even on local people. Two rates apply: one between 5.30 a.m. and 9 p.m. and the other between 9 p.m. and 5.30 a.m. By law, the driver must start the meter when you enter the car and, if requested, give you an official receipt. The best thing is to rely on the official agencies at the Gates of the Old City, or call, in the New City, the numbers below and you will be picked up in a few minutes (always specify the number of people travelling). tel. 231231/253233 or 664444/634444.

Sheruts: These shared taxis, usually eight-seater Mercedes, circulate round Jerusalem's streets on Friday evenings and Saturdays from as soon as West Jerusalem's bus service stops running until the moment it restarts. They also pick up passengers after the last bus each day. Sheruts will let you get off where you like, although they do have regular stops. You can hail one just as you can a taxi. Ask, however, before you even step in if it is, in fact, a *sherut* and not a regular taxi.

Sheruts also offer the fastest and most comfortable means of intercity travel, at fares only slightly higher than those of the bus. Except for the special Jerusalem-Ben Gurion airport run, it is not necessary to reserve seats for intercity travel. Most *sherut* booking agencies are located in side streets off Ben Yehuda Street, or at the junction of Ben Yehuda and King George V streets, as well as outside Damascus Gate. Inter-city tariffs are fixed by the government and are higher on Sabbaths and holidays and after the last buses.

Trains: A few trains leave daily except Saturdays for Tel Aviv and Haifa. For information, dial 733764.

WATER. Tap water is drinkable in Jerusalem and throughout Israel, though it is not always very tasty. Your hotel may provide you with a carafe of water. In all hotels and restaurants, and in many pharmacies, mineral waters are on sale.

SOME USEFUL EXPRESSIONS

	Hebrew	Arabic
yes/no	**ken/lo**	*náam/la*
please/thank you	**bevakashá/todá**	*lútfan/shókran*
excuse me	**slikhá**	*máthera*
Do you speak English?	**atá medabér anglít**	*btitkállem inglízi*
What does this mean?	**ma hain´y/an**	*shu máanah háda*
Waiter (Waitress), please.	**meltzár (meltzarít)**	*ya nadel*
I'd like…	**aní rotzé**	*bíddi*
How much is that?	**káma ze olé**	*háda bikám*
What time is it?	**ma hashaá**	*kam el-sáa*
Could you tell me…?	**tukhál lomár li**	*ull li*
Where are the toilets?	**eyfó hasherutím**	*fen elmaráhid*
Help me, please.	**azór li, bevakashá**	*sáedni*

Index

An asterisk (*) next to a page number indicates a map reference. For index to Practical Information.

INDEX

128